More Than a SMART GOAL

Staying Focused on Student Learning

ANNE E. Conzemius

TERRY Morganti-Fisher

Solution Tree | Press

a division of
Solution Tree

555 North Morton Street
Bloomington, IN 47404
800.733.6786 (toll free) / 812.336.7700
FAX: 812.336.7790

email: info@solution-tree.com
solution-tree.com

Printed in the United States of America

15 14 13 12 11   1 2 3 4 5

Library of Congress Cataloging-in-Publication Data

Conzemius, Anne, 1953-
  More than a SMART goal : staying focused on student learning / Anne E. Conzemius and Terry Morganti-Fisher.
     p. cm.
  Includes bibliographical references and index.
  ISBN 978-1-935543-24-4 (perfect bound) -- ISBN 978-1-935543-25-1 (library ed.) 1. School improvement programs--United States. 2. Education--Aims and objectives--United States. 3. Strategic planning--United States. I. Morganti-Fisher, Terry. II. Title.
  LB2822.82.C668 2011
  371.2'07--dc23
                              2011024302

Solution Tree
Jeffrey C. Jones, CEO & President

Solution Tree Press
President: Douglas M. Rife
Publisher: Robert D. Clouse
Vice President of Production: Gretchen Knapp
Managing Production Editor: Caroline Wise
Senior Production Editor: Lesley Bolton
Proofreader: Sarah Payne-Mills
Text Designer: Jenn Taylor
Cover Designer: Orlando Angel

Anne E. Conzemius
To my parents, OB and Polly Zimmerman, who insisted that anything worth doing is worth doing well.

Terry Morganti-Fisher
In memory of my father, Anthony Morganti, whose dedication to public education inspires me to carry on his work.

ACKNOWLEDGMENTS

Oh, the gifts we have been given.

—Terry and Anne

This book is a gift from hundreds, if not thousands, of people who have touched our lives in meaningful ways. Brushed by fate within a universe of ideas, we have been shaped by the mere act of being in the same room with you, listening on the same call or webinar with you, or reading your words along the way. Though we may not be able to attach the ideas to your names—or perhaps even know your names—it is important to us to acknowledge that we have benefited and learned from you in ways that cannot be measured but are nonetheless profound.

To the dedicated leaders and learners in our client districts who do the hard work of school improvement every day, never giving up on the endless pursuit of better outcomes for our children and youth, thank you for the gift of knowing that what we stand for and do really makes a difference.

Then there are those whose names come immediately to mind when we consider the gifts we have been given over the years. Our gratitude knows no bounds:

- To two dear friends who have supported us in so many ways—Jody Westbrook and Rich Teerlink. You have both given us the gifts of perspective, insight, and inspiration.

- To our QLD colleagues—Kiett Takkunen, Michelle Larson, Becki Kearns, Mark Zimmerman, and all of our amazing coaches and consultants. You have given us the gifts of patience and understanding in our most challenging moments.

- To our professional mentors and those who have believed in our work for many years—Shirley Hord, Stephanie Hirsh, Joellen Killion, Carol François, Bill Sommers, and Lauren Resnick. You have given us the gifts of knowledge, encouragement, and abundant resources.

- To Jan O'Neill, whose passion for student learning has never let us lose sight of what matters most—improved and improving results. You have given us the gift of unyielding commitment to stay the course.

- To our partners in life—Steven and Bill. You have given us the gifts of courage, self-sacrifice, unconditional support, and wisdom.

We especially want to acknowledge and thank the team of exceptional people who contributed directly to the writing, reviewing, and editing of this book. Our heartfelt thanks go out to:

- Shirley Hord, Linda Christensen, Kris Hipp, Pauli Nikolay, Leslie Steinhaus, and Jan O'Neill. We appreciate your candid, thoughtful feedback. We know we have a better product because of your contributions.

- Becki Kearns, whose technical competence lifted the burden of details from our shoulders so that we could concentrate on the ideas, research, and writing of this book.

- Mark Zimmerman, whose editorial contributions, project management skills, and amazing sensitivity in our *moments of truth* gave us the confidence we needed to complete this challenge.

Thank you all. It has been an extraordinary journey!

Solution Tree Press would like to thank the following reviewers:

Kim Bailey
Director, Instructional Support
  and Staff Development
Capistrano Unified School District
San Juan Capistrano, California

Barbara Bushnell
PLC Associate, Solution Tree
St. Charles, Missouri

Linda Christensen
Director of Instruction
Verona High School
Verona, Wisconsin

Debbie Fay
Principal
Mountain View Middle School
Moreno Valley, California

Sharon Kramer
Independent Consultant
Buffalo Grove, Illinois

Liz Morrison
Coordinator of Staff Development
Parkway School District
St. Louis, Missouri

Regina Owens
Administrator, Virtual School
Spring Independent School District
Spring, Texas

Geri Parscale
Deputy Superintendent
Fort Leavenworth Unified School
    District 207
Fort Leavenworth, Kansas

Ainsley Rose
Independent Consultant
Rose Educational Development
Kanata, Ontario, Canada

Heather Sanchez
Professional Development
    Specialist
Poudre School District
Fort Collins, Colorado

Teresa Songs
Principal
Chase Middle School
Topeka, Kansas

Jody Westbrook
Executive Director
Learning Forward Texas
Keller, Texas

TABLE OF CONTENTS

ABOUT THE AUTHORS

ANNE E. CONZEMIUS is cofounder and president of QLD Learning, a school improvement company headquartered in Madison, Wisconsin. Before QLD, Anne served as the assistant to Wisconsin's superintendent of public instruction; in that capacity, she worked on educational policy and led the department's strategic planning and restructuring initiative.

Earlier in her career, Anne worked as a senior associate with Howick and Associates, applying her expertise in strategic planning and quality improvement to benefit government, education, manufacturing, finance, health care, and not-for-profit organizations. From 1988 to 1990, Anne served as director of employee development and training for the state of Wisconsin. Anne has also served as a school psychologist and as a consultant with the Department of Public Instruction.

Anne is coauthor of *Building Shared Responsibility for Student Learning*, *The Handbook for SMART School Teams*, and *The Power of SMART Goals*. She has also been published in local, state, and national education newsletters and journals, and she is a contributing author to a graduate textbook on staff development.

Anne earned two master's degrees (educational psychology and industrial relations) at the University of Wisconsin–Madison. Anne and her husband, Bill, live on a farm near Madison, where they operate a horse stable and entertain their two grandsons, Quinn and Edilfanta. To learn more about Anne's work, visit QLD's website, smartlearningcommunity.net.

TERRY MORGANTI-FISHER repurposed herself through retirement after twenty-five years of service to the Austin (Texas) Independent School District to pursue continuous school improvement work on a broader scale. She has led systemic educational reform initiatives since 1989.

As director of professional development (PD) in Austin, Terry led the creation of a comprehensive PD plan and developed support systems for teacher quality. She served as district liaison to external partners, including the Institute for Learning. Terry also served the district as a special education teacher and instructional technology facilitator.

Terry is vice president of client services for QLD Learning. She is also a senior consultant for Learning Forward (formerly National Staff Development Council [NSDC]) and facilitator for the organization's Learning School Alliance. Terry is the former president of Learning Forward Texas.

Terry earned her bachelor of science in special education and elementary education at Westfield (Massachusetts) State University and her master of education in curriculum and instruction and instructional technology at the University of Texas at Austin. She is a graduate of NSDC's Academy VIII and is a certified coach. Her work has appeared in the *Journal of Staff Development*.

Terry's mission is to make the world a better place for children through public education. She lives in Austin, Texas, with her husband, Steven, and their blended family. Follow Terry via Twitter at @smartterrymf, and learn more about her work at smartlearningcommunity.net.

To book Anne E. Conzemius or Terry Morganti-Fisher for professional development, contact pd@solution-tree.com.

INTRODUCTION

The main thing is to keep the main thing the main thing.
—STEPHEN R. COVEY

When there are so many things to get done, so many people to please, and so many children in need, how can we know what matters most? Recall the advice given to Mitch Robbins (played by Billy Crystal) in the movie *City Slickers* (Smith & Underwood, 1991). While on a cattle drive in unfamiliar territory, alone in the foothills with a rather imposing and unpredictable trail boss, Robbins is advised to keep just one thing in mind. The trail boss, Curly, says that he has seen hundreds of city slickers come and go, all of them seeking respite from their world of constant worry and busyness. He tells Robbins, "None of you city folks know the secret to life," at which time, in a slow but deliberate motion, Curly raises his index finger. Robbins asks, "The secret to life is one finger?" Curly replies, "One thing, it's just one thing." "That's great, but what's the one thing?" Curly smiles and says, "You gotta figure that out."

In education, our number-one thing is student learning. That may sound simplistic and ridiculously obvious, but judging from the behavior of many of the adults involved, it's anything but the priority. In fact, in some school environments, one would wonder if the students are part of the equation at all except that *their* behaviors are so outrageous that, at a minimum, they're able to get our attention. We may want to consider whether this is a chicken-and-egg phenomenon. Has our lack of focus on learning contributed to the behaviors we're experiencing, or have the behaviors kept us from focusing on learning? It's probably a little of each. Since we don't have ultimate control over all of the factors that drive student behavior, we'll focus on the things over which we have the most control: the conditions within which learning takes place.

At its core, this book is about learning—organizational, team, and student learning. It's about the conditions that educators control and the actions, decisions, and attitudes they impose on the learning environment that either support or diminish learning potential. To be more specific, the focus is on learning, not achievement. Achievement is an end point (for example, the achievement of a goal) or evidence that learning has occurred (for example, a test score or a performance well done). It is one of many indicators of success. Though important, it's only part of the story and may not even verify that learning has occurred. It is possible for a student to achieve success on a task or a test and walk away having learned little, as judged by the student's ability to apply the achievement to a new context or to solving a new problem. A simple example is spelling a list of words correctly on a weekly spelling test and then misspelling or misusing the same words in a written essay. Another example is learning how to solve an algebraic equation but not being able to create or solve one related to a real-life situation. It's also possible to have acquired a tremendous amount of new knowledge without having learned its value with regard to real-life decisions or applications. Learning and achievement are both important; neither is sufficient without the other.

Learning is an active, ongoing, and lifelong process that adds value to individual lives, organizational cultures, communities, global societies, and the human race. Learning engages the entire being—mind, body, and spirit. It is inherently neutral. Though the content of the learning may be politically charged or maliciously motivated, the act of learning is neither. Learning fuels growth, unleashes potential, and spawns creativity. It is not necessarily content specific. It engages all of our intelligences (Gardner, 1993) and, as such, plays an important role in everything we do throughout our lives, whether we're in a classroom, in an office, at a park, in a place of worship, or at home.

Benchmarking Best Practices

We understand that education is unique and special in many ways. We recognize the formidable challenges that this very public enterprise must overcome in pursuit of its important mission. We know that educators lack sufficient control over their own destiny because, while funding is not within their control, the doors must remain open to all. Of course, we would not begin to suggest that we abandon our mission, our open-door policies, or our very successful practices. We need to celebrate the work of the millions of dedicated people over the centuries who have provided life-enriching educational opportunities for all.

We recognize that life, both inside and outside the walls of educational institutions, is constantly changing. However, we also recognize the implicit rejection of opportunities by educators to learn from other industries that are experiencing the same or similar changes. We are not saying that others know better. In fact, in some cases, educators know best and have much to share beyond our walls. We are saying that there are concepts, tools, and methods that are proven effective across industry lines because they are unaffected by content or context. They address ubiquitous concerns, are designed to facilitate broad-based understanding, apply to universal principles, and have stood the tests of multiple applications over decades.

Many of the tools and concepts in this book are rooted in statistical theory and practice. They can be applied to almost any kind of data and do not require a PhD in mathematics to understand or use. Some are designed specifically for collaborative use by educators (such as professional learning communities, groups, committees, task forces, and boards) to facilitate understanding. Others are designed to bring focus, clarity, and organization to the work itself. These tools and methods have been shamelessly borrowed from multiple industries where their use has led to documented success in organizational, team, and individual learning.

Table I.1 lists some of these concepts, tools, and methods and where they are currently being used in education with great success. Our goal is to augment their use, encourage broader application and deeper understanding of their use, and add new tools to the educator's toolbox, all in the name of improving organizational, team, and student learning.

Table I.1: Current Educational Applications of Best Practices in Business

Business Practices	Educational Applications
Common versus special cause variation	Curriculum articulation and alignment Common core standards
80/20 rule (Pareto principle)	SMART goals
Learning organization	Professional learning communities Collaborative teams Mission, vision, and values
Benchmarking	Best-practice research
Data-driven decision making	Continuous school improvement Action research SMART goals process Walkthroughs Assessment for learning

There are additional tools and concepts that are in the early stages of use in education, including value-added research, performance dashboards, cause-and-effect analyses, and return on investment (ROI). These tools and concepts are especially useful for leaders, but they can also be applied at any level of the organization or even to individual situations. Finally, understanding the use and interpretation of run and control charts, the Pareto principle, and the SMART Goal Tree Diagram™ will assist teams and individuals at all levels, resulting in better decisions, more effective actions, and the communication of their learning to broader audiences with clarity and confidence.

A Word About Words

Words are our friends. They help us communicate our most intimate thoughts, our deepest feelings, and our wildest dreams. They also help us build relationships, explain our intentions, and create understanding. As educators, we are masters of words. We speak fluently in a language filled with words and terms that are all our own—*rubrics*, *taxonomies*, *innovation configurations*, and *pedagogy* to name a few. These are ideas that are known to us but are rarely used outside of the educational domain. Then there are the ever-popular acronyms that we toss about freely—PLCs, SMART goals, EL, RTI, and so on. These are our secret codes. They are useful to us on a daily basis and simplify our internal oral and written communication processes. We also use words that describe what might be considered commonly understood ideals and strategies such as *collaboration*, *accountability*, *standards*, and *achievement*. Most people have at least a notion about what these mean, yet each has its own interpretation within the context of its use.

We will use words in this book that are familiar to educators and some that are unfamiliar. To be clear, even those that are familiar require some definition so as not to confuse the reader who may experience them or know them only within their unique context.

Professional Learning Communities

We acknowledge and are grateful for the tremendous contributions that the experts—Richard and Rebecca DuFour, Robert Eaker, Shirley Hord, Kris Hipp, Fred Newmann, and Gary Wehlage—have brought to our understanding of what it means to create and truly engage in professional learning communities (PLCs). We are aware that the use of the PLC acronym is being applied differently across the education community. Some refer to grade-level or department teams as PLCs; some describe ad hoc study groups or dialogue sessions as PLCs; and others speak more broadly as they refer to their entire system as a PLC. While each of the experts views it slightly differently, for the most part, there is consensus that a PLC is *a community of professionals engaged in an ongoing process of learning together for the purpose of improving their practice in support of better results for students.* In this book, the school is the focus for PLCs, and we refer to grade-level and department teams as collaborative teams and study and dialogue groups as learning teams.

Data

It's amazing the effect this little four-letter word has on people. For some, the use of data is akin to breathing—how could we possibly live without it? For others, data are seen as nothing less than life-threatening. Perhaps more than any other word in the current education vernacular, *data* conjures emotional reactions along the fullest and most complex continuum. The emotions derive from one's experience, expertise, and the historical or perceived consequences associated with its use. For those who find data to be an essential part of life, their experiences and understandings have led to better decisions and a sense of predictability or confidence. But for those who have experienced the use of data as uncomfortably revealing or the precursor to some real or perceived punishment, the fear can be gripping.

There are two distinctions we want to make about the use of data in professional practice. The first speaks to the emotional side, the second to the technical side. First, we believe that data should be viewed as information gathered in pursuit of understanding and learning for improvement. On its own, that seems fairly objective. Emotions come into the picture when there is either a celebration of the results or a negative consequence that is endured following an analysis or interpretation of the data. Neither would necessarily be considered an appropriate response to the data, regardless of its source or intended application. For example, pairing a single year's test scores on high-stakes achievement measures with sanctions or rewards not only heightens the likelihood of fear-based tampering but, from a policy perspective, is analogous to investing in magic potions. Celebrations are a good thing but need to be associated with real and intentional change, not a single year of upturn on a run chart.

Second, from a practical point of view, when we use the term *data*, we are referring to a host of data sources and types:

1. Qualitative (for example, people's perceptions and feelings)

2. Quantitative (for example, scores, statistical calculations, and summations derived from observations or recorded facts, such as attendance or referral rates)

3. Intuitive (for example, the data we gather from paying attention to our experiences, values, and sensory inputs)

In this book, we reference all of the preceding sources and types, believe each serves a unique and important purpose, and accept all three as equally valuable in the decision-making process.

Leaders and Leadership

Wherever we use the word *leader*, unless otherwise specified, we are referring to any individual in the organization who is empowered to act with authority to make decisions with students and on behalf of students. Leaders include the official positions of leadership in the organization (central office personnel and school-based leaders such as principals, assistant principals and deans, department heads, and grade-level teacher leaders) but are not limited just to positions. As we seek to build leadership capacity throughout the system, we open the door for leadership to become the domain of every person within the system, including students: everyone a learner, everyone a leader.

Leadership is the actions taken by those who choose to lead, whether it is leadership within a classroom, a PLC, a school improvement team, a parent advisory team, or the student body. We are especially fond of the way in which Linda Lambert (1998) talks about leadership as "the reciprocal learning process that enables participants in a community to construct meaning toward a shared purpose" (p. 18).

Improvement and Innovation

We turn to the work of Robert Davidovich, Pauli Nikolay, Bonnie Laugerman, and Carol Commodore (2010) to help us distinguish between these two essential concepts. Improvement is about getting better; innovation is about becoming different. Improvement can happen incrementally or as a breakthrough extension of current practice either made better or applied more effectively within the realm of a present-day standard. Innovation occurs either in the absence of an existing strategy or as a completely new approach to several, previously unconnected strategies. It creates "new dimensions of performance" (Davidovich et al., 2010, p. 28) and results in entirely new capacities or solutions. Davidovich and his coauthors (2010) assert, "The important challenge facing educational leaders at all levels is to realize that improving and innovating are both necessary and that both need to be part of their leadership repertoire" (p. 24).

We struggled with this distinction as it applies to the ideas we share in this book. Most of our work is and has been in the realm of improvement. However, we also recognize that improvement is not always sufficient and that it is not exclusive of innovation. Let's use a familiar object to illustrate the difference between improvement and innovation—the telephone.

Initially, the telephone was invented as a tool for oral communication between two individuals (albeit often on a party line where others could eavesdrop unnoticed). As the telephone system was improved, it became more private (the party lines were abandoned), and the phone itself became easier to use (push button versus rotary dial, remote handsets to allow for freedom of movement, headsets for hands-free applications) with many more features to enhance its use (conference capabilities, speakers, caller ID, and telecommunications devices for the deaf, to name a few). All of these changes would be categorized as improvements. Individually and collectively, they have made the telephone better. These improvements represent valuable changes to a fundamentally unchanged tool.

Now, ask anyone between the ages of ten and twenty what a telephone is and does, and you'll get a very different description of a very different set of features and benefits. Communication is still an inherent value, but technology innovations are driving the use of this tool to a completely different place. The fundamental purpose and use of phones have been redefined, and in many cases, the smartphone has replaced the telephone. Smartphone technologies are now improving at a rapid rate and will, no doubt, be replaced with yet another innovation for enhanced communication in the not-too-distant future. The important thing to remember is that, though the tool has changed, the need for it (communication) has not. For our purposes, schools are the tool, and learning is the need.

In our telephone example, both improvement and innovation have a place in the process of change. The key to knowing which to pursue is a function of urgency, the changing environment within which the customer (student) must thrive, and the magnitude of the gap that needs to be closed. With regard to the tools and methods outlined in this book, it is our hope that the reader sees them as applicable and useful, whether the best strategy is deemed to be an improvement or innovation.

Chaos

Chaos is not a problem. In fact, chaos can be a good thing. It is the disequilibrium that is needed for innovation to occur (Davidovich et al., 2010; Wheatley, 1992): "The things we fear most in organizations—fluctuations, disturbances, imbalances—need not be signs of an impending disorder that will destroy us. Instead, fluctuations are the primary source of creativity" (Wheatley, 1992, p. 20). In this context, chaos is both a natural and healthy contributor to the process of innovation.

Stability Versus Rigidity

An unstable system is one in which results vary dramatically from one point in time to another without apparent reason. The first step in a continuous improvement process is to bring stability to the system. This is done by creating norms and standards, bringing coherence to major delivery systems (such as the curriculum), and defining a common aim, mission, or purpose for the system. When the system is brought into balance, it becomes possible to measure the impact of improvement strategies, giving those involved in the process the information and focus needed to make good decisions. System stability does not preclude the design of highly creative means for improving performance. Innovative solutions and approaches to improvement can greatly enhance performance outcomes, but ultimately, in order to know whether an innovation has been successful, it must be implemented, measured, and improved within the context of the system's purpose or aim. This is the cycle of continuous improvement that brings stability and balance back to the system.

Rigidity, on the other hand, is a state of inflexibility that limits potential and defies innovation and improvement. A rigid system limits the amount of new data that can enter or be distributed throughout the system. A culture of rigidity will seek to deny, suppress, interpret, or control the new information in a way that maintains the status quo. In a system or culture that is rigid, compliance is king because new data, creative thinking, and innovation are not welcome. Unless the culture changes to one that values and incorporates the introduction, use, and distribution of new data on an ongoing basis (continuous improvement), the system will atrophy, and results will decline.

Simple Versus Simplicity

One of our favorite sayings is from Oliver Wendell Holmes Jr.: "I wouldn't give a fig for the simplicity on this side of complexity, but I would give my life for the simplicity on the other side of complexity" (www.wikiquote.org). When we're on the upside of a learning or creativity curve, our tendency is to begin with a simplistic understanding or a simple idea that seems like a no-brainer to make happen. Even Geoffrey Canada in *Waiting for "Superman"* (Chilcott & Guggenheim, 2010) admits that he knew exactly what needed to happen to reform education and figured he alone would have it taken care of in two to three years. But, as they say, the devil is in the details, and as we move more deeply into understanding a new piece of knowledge or comprehending the strength of the system that is holding the innovation back, we quickly get overwhelmed with managing the complexity. As we work our way through, we begin to see connections. We begin to assimilate the important aspects of the new learning or applications of the new idea, and an elegant simplicity emerges. That is simplicity on the other side of complexity.

To illustrate this process, let's start with just one new initiative. It is introduced as simply a new way to teach X. With little or no time designated for learning how to teach X, most people tend to dive right in and give it a try. It isn't long before it doesn't feel so simple anymore, at which time the initiative is either abandoned or another one comes along. With multiple initiatives coming and going, it is easy to see how we become caught in complexity, never to get to the other side. Our hope is that the tools and methods presented in this book will help educators move beyond and through complexity to find not simplistic solutions but elegant simplicity.

About the Book

Certain assumptions have guided us in selecting the tools and methods presented in this book. To the extent that the reader agrees with these assumptions, the tools and methods we offer will be useful and rational.

Where there is doubt, we ask only that you consider the possibility that they have merit, and then give the tools and methods a try. The following assumptions are not presented in any particular order of importance. Each assumption addresses a unique and fundamental set of beliefs that constitute the theoretical foundation for our improvement work with schools.

- Assumption #1: One must first understand that which one seeks to improve.
- Assumption #2: Strategic focus improves results.
- Assumption #3: Engagement is a key factor in learning.
- Assumption #4: Structures and processes affect performance.
- Assumption #5: Continuous feedback is the engine for improvement.
- Assumption #6: Leadership matters.

Chapter 1: The Nature of Systems Improvement

Much has been written about the nature of systems (Buffum, Mattos, & Weber, 2009; Davidovich et al., 2010; Dolan, 1994; Fullan, 1991; Hall & Hord, 2011; Schlechty, 1991; Senge, 1990; Wheatley, 1992), yet we continue to struggle with finding a formula that really works when it comes to educational reform. The good news is that there are known and commonly understood methodologies that foster deep change and improved learning. In this chapter, we highlight the five guidelines for creating a robust methodology that engages the entire system in the change process. The data generated from the implementation of this methodology ultimately become the evidence used in later chapters to monitor and document the success of any organizational improvement effort. We also examine the elements of system improvement that need to be in place for sustainable, positive change to occur and explore three different types of improvement approaches.

Chapter 2: Less Is More

Chapter 2 is all about getting and staying focused on what matters most. We explore a variety of ways to do so, including the use of reflection as an essential professional practice. Reflection on data, reflection on goals, and reflection on practice are all ways to minimize the noise often caused by too many disconnected initiatives. This chapter will give meaning to the many adages lauding the value of a simpler way.

In our work with schools, we have observed tomes of district planning and school improvement documents that contain dozens of vague pro forma goals that rarely see the light of day after they are written. The proliferation of goals often has more to do with what is mandated than what is truly desired. When schools have dozens of goals, what they end up with is a lot of programmatic start-ups, a lot of activity, and ultimately a lot of exhausted people with little or no long-term benefit for students. Is it possible to have too much of a good thing? When is less really more?

In our experience, setting a single SMART (strategic and specific, measurable, attainable, results oriented, and time bound) goal that addresses a deeply rooted cause, created in a way that garners the commitment of the entire faculty, has a much higher probability of resulting in improvement. That's often a tough sell. School leaders sometimes begin the goal-writing process confident that the school should be focusing on one particular subject but find, once they've looked at the data, that their greatest need is in another.

In chapter 2, we share a data-analysis process that schools are using to identify their greatest area of need (GAN). The GAN creates the singular focus for the school's SMART goal. GAN is based on the Pareto principle, which is the underlying concept of SMART and why SMART works. The process of finding the GAN and then building the SMART goal from the data creates schoolwide focus and coherence in goal setting and monitoring. It is also the fundamental process and tool for bringing focus to the work of PLCs, grade-level and department collaborative teams, classroom instruction, professional development, and student-focused interventions for RTI plans.

Chapter 3: Putting SMART Goals to Work

One might argue that the exercise of writing the goal is sufficient. There is tremendous intrinsic value in goal development. Think about a time in your life when you set a goal. What did having that goal do for you? Did it bring energy? Did it create clarity and focus? Did it give you direction? Did you feel accountable for achieving it? Goals are so much more than a simple statement of intent. They fuel motivation and communicate value. They are a public declaration of what is both important and desired.

Having a goal and using the goal are not one and the same. In chapter 3, we link the intrinsic motivational qualities of the goal-writing experience to the actions that move the organization toward its preferred outcomes. Making SMART goals integral to the larger school and district improvement process and engaging people in that process are key aspects of getting results. In this chapter, we explore the leadership roles that are needed to facilitate the integration and the participation of the broader school community.

Ultimately, it is not until students themselves are setting and monitoring their own learning goals that the power of the goal-setting process is realized. We include stories of how students of all ages are using data to set and monitor their own SMART learning goals and the impact it is having on their lives.

Chapter 4: Professional Learning by Design

High-performing schools create the time and place for teachers to engage in dynamic conversations about data, goal setting, and instructional improvement, and the expectation that they will do so. These conversations are at the foundation of job-embedded professional learning. When structures and processes exist to support professional learning, the outcomes are qualitatively and quantitatively better than those any mandate for improvement could achieve. That's because the conversations occur within a community in which teachers learn together as they pursue their common goal.

It's one thing to have a personal goal, which may or may not be shared with someone else. It's quite another for a group of people, a team, or an organization to have and pursue a common goal. The process of agreeing on what the goal should be and how bold or ambitious it should be is a challenge in the healthiest of circumstances, which is why it doesn't just happen. We know that when educators collaboratively engage in a process for goal setting and goal attainment, and everyone involved knows what to expect and how to proceed, the challenges associated with setting the goal diminish. The appropriate structures and processes need to be in place so that the conversations will lead to shared responsibility for meeting the goal.

Chapter 5: Impact and Implementation

Three simple questions guide every decision that is made about improving conditions for learning:

1. Are we getting the results we want?

2. Are we staying focused on what matters most?

3. Is everyone in the system contributing to the accomplishment of the mission?

These three questions are addressed in chapter 5. They provide the framework for understanding, measuring, and improving our ability to support learning at the classroom, team, campus, and district levels. It almost doesn't matter what programs a district has chosen to resource its learning. There are thousands from which to choose, and most of them have some track record of success. What does matter is that there is an all-out, wholesale commitment to a common, strategic direction and that there is a system in place for making sure that everyone is involved in moving the organization in that direction. It matters that people believe in the chosen initiative or program so that it can be implemented with fidelity. It matters that there is a system in place for measuring the success of the initiative or program and that success has to do with student learning, not the ease of the initiative's or program's use by the adults in the system. Finally, it matters that all voices are listened to, not just heard, and that includes the voices of students and their parents.

We have developed and implemented a process and set of tools used at the system level to monitor the implementation effectiveness of any goal-driven intervention or initiative. The SMART Measurement System™ (SMS™) is based on multiple sources of data—both quantitative and qualitative—which combine to show evidence of change over time. In this chapter, we share the tools and processes of the SMS. Through the use of this system on an iterative basis throughout the year, district and school-based leaders are able to monitor whether their investment of resources is being effectively deployed, allowing them to make data-based decisions on how best to protect and support that investment over the long term and assure their return on investment.

Chapter 6: Engaging the Mind, Body, and Spirit

Ultimately, systemic reform is a human endeavor, not an organizational exercise. The work that has been laid out in this book is not the work of one person. It cannot be done by a single leader or even a leadership team. It is, at its core, a *shared responsibility* model. Effective leaders of reform understand that building leadership capacity is the key to sustainable improvement.

Some leaders are better at this kind of leadership than others. Leaders who themselves are unfocused, prone to flavor-of-the-month initiatives, ego-driven, overly influenced by the politics of their role, or dependent on the next guru who walks through the door are doing us more harm than good, no matter how competent they may be at the pragmatic side of the business of change. The nature of systemic reform requires leaders with vision and visibility, a balance of urgency and patience, and the ability to direct when direction is needed and then to let go at just the right time. We need leaders who understand how to build trust, establish authentic relationships, communicate in coherent and focused ways, and lead by example.

Building trust is a significant part of establishing and sustaining the relationships needed to create leadership capacity. When leaders behave in ways that are consistent with their words and stated values, when they follow through on commitments and stay the course of the vision, and when they engage others fully in the change process, trust becomes the by-product of their leadership—and that trust goes a long way toward breaking down resistance to change.

CHAPTER 1

The Nature of Systems Improvement

See it big, and keep it simple.

—WILFERD PETERSON

Years ago, Anne took advantage of an opportunity to spend some quality time with her younger brother—and get a free golf lesson. Rob was a card-carrying Professional Golfers' Association of America (PGA) member and the head teaching pro at Honey Bee Golf Course in Virginia Beach.

As they headed to the driving range, Rob quizzed her: "Why do you play golf, and where do you see golf in your future? How important is it in terms of your life goals?"

Anne responded dutifully: "I play because it's fun. I don't have plans to join the pro circuit, and it's only mildly important to me because it demands more time than I have to give it right now."

Once they reached the range, Anne thought that if she just started swinging, Rob would have to stop asking questions, but he persisted. "Just a little more background will be helpful. What is your typical score? What would you say are the strongest and weakest points of your game? How good do you want to get?"

Anne acquiesced: "Bogey, distance, approach, and good enough not to embarrass myself—in that order."

It was finally time to tee it up and swing. Rob observed, took notes, walked around, and said, "Well, if you want to get substantially better, we're going to need to work on your whole swing. If you want to get a little bit better, I can give you some easy tips to improve your score. What do you think?" Anne smiled and said, "I think it's time for a beer."

You don't have to be a golfer to learn from this lesson. What Anne's brother understood was that golf, like any dynamic system, can be improved if we know fundamentally what we want from the game and why we're playing it. These are questions of vision and purpose (or mission). He also knew that, in order to improve, we need to know what our current and typical system is producing—scores, strengths, weaknesses, and accuracy. Finally, in order to select the most appropriate teaching approach, he needed to know how good was good enough from Anne's perspective—in other words, her goal. Implicit in his series of questions was an underlying methodology for examining her system of golf. As a teacher, he needed to understand the context she brought to the game. Only then could he truly understand where to begin to help her.

Methodology: One Big Idea, Five Simple Guidelines

Asking questions about purpose, vision, and goals is a great way to begin the system-improvement conversation. The following guidelines take that conversation further, comprising a methodology for system improvement that is informed by data and characterized by the full and active engagement of the people within the system.

The First Guideline

Understand the aim of the system before you set out to improve it.

According to Davidovich et al. (2010), a system refers to interrelated, independent entities that form a complex, unified whole. The interdependent entities work together to try to accomplish a particular aim. The aim defines the system's reason for being and gives those inside the system a sense of purpose. A system must have an aim. Without an aim, there is no system (Deming, 1993).

As we consider schools and their structures to improve student learning, we must examine the interrelated nature of the component parts of the organization, the core delivery processes, and the interdependent relationships between and among the people and their tasks. In the case of a school system, the aim answers various questions at multiple levels of the organization:

- Why does this school exist?
- What is the purpose of professional learning communities?
- Why is this important for me or us to learn?
- Why do I come to school each day?

Understanding the aim of the system brings coherence to the actions taken within the system. W. Edwards Deming (1986) refers to this in *Out of the Crisis* as *constancy of purpose.*

Knowing why the system exists and what it is meant to do is fundamental to system improvement. How else could we know if we're doing the right things? Even if we're doing things well, if those things don't contribute to our purpose, then why are we doing them at all? How can we determine whether our actions and decisions align with our purpose? Alignment exists when "a group of people function as a whole. . . . The fundamental characteristic of the relatively unaligned team [organization in this case] is wasted energy" (Senge, 1990, p. 234). Though individuals in an unaligned team may be working extraordinarily hard, their efforts do not efficiently translate to better results for the team, the school, or the system as a whole.

A mission statement is a statement of purpose. It communicates the reason the organization currently exists and why it was created in the first place. Most schools and even some classrooms have mission statements. As Richard DuFour and Robert Eaker (1998) point out, school mission statements are fairly similar from one school to the next, and though they are publically displayed and beautifully presented on walls, stationery, and business cards, they have little impact on what actually happens in the school. That's because simply having a statement will not shape behavior. Rarely does having a mission statement translate into the kind of shared understanding and commitment to the aim of the system that Deming is talking about when he refers to constancy of purpose.

The Second Guideline

Know what you want an improved system to produce or do.

What will the system be like when it's at its best? What do we expect it to accomplish? At the district level, the desired end is often called "shared vision," and at the classroom level, "a common set of standards." Regardless of the organizational level or the terms used, knowing what is needed from the system gives guidance to how the system is designed, measured, and improved.

Stephen Covey's (1989) first habit of effectiveness is "Begin with the end in mind":

> To begin with the end in mind means to start with a clear understanding of your destination. It means to know where you're going so that you better understand where you are now and so that the steps you take are always in the right direction. (p. 98)

The proliferation of initiatives that characterize so many improvement plans and efforts is proof that the hard work of defining the end result has not been done. Each initiative seems to carry its own end point, sometimes meeting up with that of another, most likely due to randomness. If we hope to bring balance and coherence into our systems, we must be clear about the destination from the get-go.

It's difficult enough to begin with the end in mind from an individual perspective, but how does an entire organization like a school district, school, or professional learning community begin to cultivate and then pursue a shared vision or a common set of standards? The answer is: one conversation at a time. Underneath the vision is a set of assumptions, a set of values and beliefs, and a personal vision that reflects the desires and preferences of each person in the organization. By convening dialogue sessions and professional learning opportunities, taking time for reflection and conversation, the shared vision and common standards begin to emerge. There are many wonderful techniques and processes for doing this work (Conzemius & O'Neill, 2002; Garmston & Wellman, 1999; Hord, Roussin, & Sommers, 2010; Lezotte & McKee, 2002; Munger & von Frank, 2010; Saphier & D'Auria, 1993). The most important thing is to assure that these kinds of conversations are expected to happen and that time is made available for them to occur.

The Third Guideline

Understand the performance of the system over time.

When we look at data over time, we can tell a great deal about the health or effectiveness of our systems. By gathering and analyzing various types of data over multiple time periods (for example, years, semesters, quarters, weeks, or days), we can begin to see patterns emerge. These patterns provide insights into the balance, predictability, and efficiency of our systems.

The more statistically stable the system, the easier it is to understand it and improve it. Statistical stability means that there is minimal *random* variation—that is, uncontrollable or unexplainable change in results from one measurement event to the next. Because systems are dynamic and ever-changing, there will always be some variation. If there is a small amount of variation or if the variation is predictable, then the system is said to be stable or *in control*. In this case, the small amount of change in data over time can be explained by the consistent, recurring, and common factors associated with what's being measured. If the variation produces a clear trend line from one year or one measurement event to the next over multiple periods, the probability that the particular intervention being evaluated has had either a positive or negative effect increases with each subsequent and sequential data point. If there is a great deal of variation that cannot be explained, then the system is said to be unstable or *out of control*. In this case, little can be concluded about the effects of an intervention unless, of course, the intervention is meant to create dissonance or uncertainty. If there is no variation, the medical equivalent would be *flatlined*. In that case, the horse is dead. Dismount.

The amount and type of variation in a system provide clues about the best way to improve it. There are two forms of variation: (1) common cause and (2) special cause. Common cause variation occurs when many small factors continuously affect the outcomes of the system. Because these factors are present all of the time in relatively predictable sequences, the outcomes or results tend to be similar or at least close to the same over time. They may vary by a few points from one incident to the next, but they produce a fairly small range of data values on an ongoing basis, as shown on the control chart in figure 1.1 (page 20).

A system with common cause variation is stable. That's a good thing if it means that a new intervention or innovation has been successfully implemented and has brought the system to a higher level of performance overall. However, if it means that the status quo is prevailing in a culture where dramatically different results are desired, then there needs to be a fundamental shift. Tweaking many small factors will not fundamentally change the outcomes. So, if we decide that we want significantly different outcomes (for example, a bold new vision, higher standards, or big bodacious goals), or we

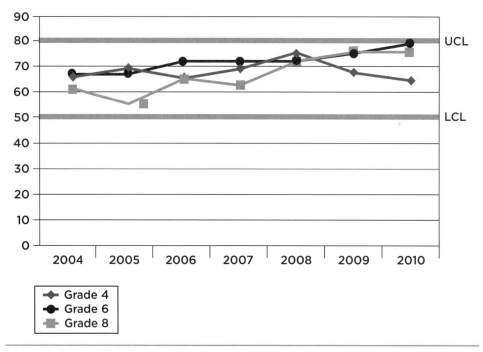

Figure 1.1: A system with common cause variation.

decide to change the aim of the system (for example, preparing students for 21st century skills), then we need to make a fundamentally strategic change. Unless the vast majority of the people in the system are deeply committed to the new vision, standards, goals, or aim, it is nothing more than wishful thinking to expect that they will voluntarily make significant changes to what seems to be working well (O'Neill, 2008).

The second type of variation—special cause—occurs when something out of the ordinary happens. It shows up in the data as an extreme data point, either much higher or much lower than the others. An example of special cause is a dramatic change in the performance of a class on a weekly quiz when taken during homecoming week. That would be an explainable change.

When analyzing for special cause, there are certain statistical thresholds, called upper control limit (UCL) and lower control limit (LCL), above or below which the data must fall to qualify as *special*. However, even the untrained eye can see a single event that is dramatically different than the rest without conducting sophisticated statistical analyses, as shown in figure 1.2.

The improvement strategy for special cause variation is to try to determine what was different. If it is explainable and not likely to occur again, ignore it (unless, of course, the cause represents a safety issue). If it is something that

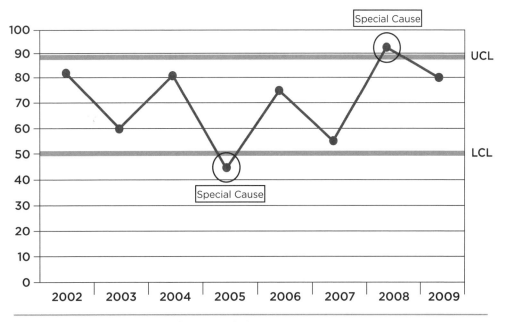

Figure 1.2: A system with special cause variation.

is within your control to change, change it. The important thing is to not overreact or change everything based on that single data point.

What happens when there is an overreaction to a single special cause? It's called tampering, and it results in the system being thrown into chaos. The proliferation of initiatives is a perfect example of tampering with the system. We don't like what we see, so we toss a solution into the mix, which, in turn, distracts or polarizes the people who love the solutions they already have. Results get worse, so we toss another initiative into the mix, and the beat goes on. Eventually, there is no predictability, no consistency, and little opportunity to improve that which is now completely out of control.

One does not have to be statistically savvy to apply the logic of using data to manage variation. Without knowing about the statistical concept, Shannon, a sixth-grade teacher, intuitively applied the theory of special cause variation in her classroom in an attempt to bring greater consistency and predictability to her teaching and to her students' learning. Here's what she did. After each spelling quiz on Friday, Shannon plotted the class average on a large wall chart in time order (a run chart), so that when the students returned on Monday morning, they could see how they had done. What Shannon didn't know at the time was that she was using data as a tool to better understand her system of teaching spelling. What she did know was that the results were closely correlated with the students' behaviors the following week. It seemed that when they did poorly one week, they ramped up their studying and did better the next week. Conversely, when they did well, they slacked off the following week. She wondered if the results were affecting their motivation or if their motivation was affecting the results; given that these were sixth graders, it was also possible that it had mostly to do with hormones. At any rate, the class was experiencing variation.

When put to the statistical test for special cause variation, there were two particular incidences that stood out. They were explainable causes that were not in Shannon's control, so she decided not to worry about or celebrate either one. However, Shannon was not satisfied with the overall performance of the class and was unsettled by the lack of predictability that this unstable system was producing. In response, she introduced a fundamental change in her system of teaching spelling. She asked her students to brainstorm three areas of improvement:

1. What could she do differently as their teacher to help them improve?

2. What could they do differently that would help them improve?

3. What could their parents do to help them improve?

As a class, they selected a few of the ideas from each category and compiled them to create a compact that was signed by every student, his or her parents, and Shannon. They standardized their system for improvement. After several weeks, the data were clear—two different kinds of improvement were happening. Not only was the overall class performance on the weekly quizzes improving, as shown on the run chart in figure 1.3, but there was far less variation in performance from week to week. No doubt, there were additional motivational and behavioral benefits as well.

Seeing the data and analyzing their variation doesn't always tell you what to do about it. In this case, Shannon didn't know for sure what was causing the changes in the data, but being an experienced and intuitive teacher, she had some reasonable best guesses about what she and the students could do differently. By engaging the students in the process of identifying the strategies, she created shared ownership and commitment to the change.

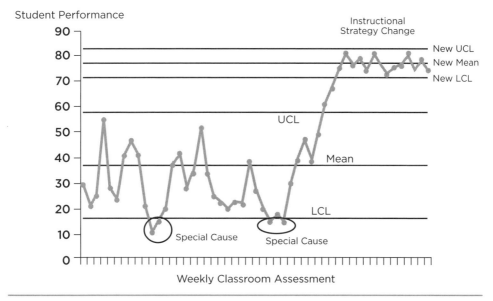

Figure 1.3: Weekly spelling-test results for Shannon's classroom.

The Fourth Guideline

Understand what is causing the system to perform as it does.

Determining causal relationships in a system requires a level of methodological rigor that is beyond the scope of most organizations. Empirical research methods that incorporate control groups in longitudinal studies are not widely acceptable when the subject matter is children and their learning. That kind of research is best left to the research institutions that have the means, the knowledge, and the general agreement of the public to employ such methods.

In the absence of carefully designed experiments, there are tools that are useful for identifying possible causal relationships in an attempt to understand the system at a deeper level. These tools tap into the experience, intuition, and good judgment of the people who have been working *in* the system for a while. Teachers, principals, students, and parents all experience the system in different ways but often come away with very similar frustrations and notions about what is causing those frustrations. Because they are *in* it every day, they sense the rhythm of the system, which stirs and motivates the desire for change when things aren't going the way the people think they should.

A cause-and-effect diagram (Conzemius & O'Neill, 2002), an example of which is shown in figure 1.4, is a tool that captures the collective experience of the people in the system in a structured way, using a series of analyses aimed at understanding why a problem exists. The participants examine possible causes or contributing factors at deeper and deeper levels as they pursue the causal chain. If the possible causes show up in a variety of categories, it's likely that the group is honing in on a systemic problem. If the possible causes are contributing to one category but are manifested in many different ways, then it's possible that the group is honing in on a specific problem or cause related to that category of system issues. In either case, this step is always followed by the collection of data to verify whether their perceptions have merit.

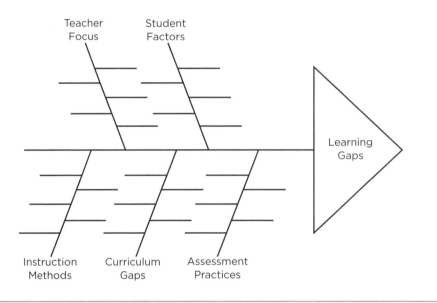

Figure 1.4: Cause-and-effect diagram.

The cause-and-effect tool, when used to analyze potential root causes, gives guidance to the data we gather, the decisions we make, and the strategies or solutions we select. Unfortunately, it is rare that a school or district will take the time to conduct a thorough analysis of potential root causes prior to determining which, if any, intervention is needed. An example of what can happen when this important step is skipped is illustrated in the following story. A district determined that they had a problem with student learning because there weren't enough computers to go around (a solution disguised as an implied root cause). The obvious solution, then, was to provide a laptop for every teacher and student in the district. The elaborate phase-in plan involved purchasing and keeping track of thousands of laptops and training students in their use. The plan was ambitious but lacked substance, context, and ultimately impact. There was no commensurate change in how the laptops were used for instruction or learning. There was no clearly articulated aim or purpose for their use. There was no system in place to measure the amount or type of use by students or teachers and certainly no system for measuring impact on student learning. Finally, the phase-in approach assured that the laptops would be obsolete before anyone could figure out what to do with them. However, the bigger issue in this case was not that there were thousands of computers hanging around, but that the real problem was never diagnosed and, therefore, not resolved. Had they taken the time and effort to dig more deeply into why students were not performing well on the application of 21st century skills, they might have discovered that the root cause had more to do with teachers' limited use of modern research and applied technologies, which, in turn, was due to their comfort level and skills in this arena. There may have been far more effective and less expensive ways to solve that problem, but they will likely never know.

The Fifth Guideline

Use a systemwide collaborative process to establish and pursue a goal that is strategic and specific, measurable, attainable, results oriented, and time bound (SMART), aimed at eliminating or mitigating the root causes.

System improvement necessitates a systemic focus and, ultimately, the alignment of actions throughout the system designed to achieve the system's goal(s). The SMART goal reflects the collective aspirations of the system as a whole, related to its aim and targeted at the underlying root causes of the system's inability to fulfill its mission.

One aspect of being strategic is the ability to think longer term and stay the course over time. Goals that reach out beyond a year are more strategic than those that focus on short-term change. However, setting a long-term goal doesn't ensure that the people or the organization will behave strategically in managing the pursuit of the goal. What is needed is a systemwide SMART process during which schools, teacher teams, and the organization as a whole think and act strategically—together. Such a process engages all parties in building coherence, alignment, focus, and direction into their goals and into the work that is aimed at achieving those goals and eliminating the systemic root causes of unacceptable academic performance. Without a SMART process, "what we end up with is individual parts of the system (schools, grade levels, department, or course-specific teams) doing their own thing in random, unconnected ways. That's not much different than the status quo" (Conzemius, 2010, p. 36).

A common root cause of chronic or systemic low performance is the lack of alignment of goals throughout the organization. There are two types of alignment, each of which is critical to the district's overall improvement efforts. The first addresses goals that link and support each other up and down the organizational structures. For example, the campus goals need to support and lead to the accomplishment of the district's strategic goals, and grade-level or department team goals need to support and lead to the accomplishment of the school's goals. Similarly, goals at the elementary school level should support and lead to the accomplishment of goals at the middle school level and ultimately to goals at the high school level. This is referred to as vertical alignment and is comparable to the work that districts do to align their curriculum from one grade level to the next.

The second type of alignment is horizontal. In this case, goals support and link across the organization in two ways. One way is by grade level or department across the system. For districts with more than one school at each level (elementary, middle, or high school), horizontal alignment would occur in such a way that grade-level or content-area teachers in the system share, discuss, and align their goals in support of all students at their grade level or in their content area. In one K–8 Illinois district with three elementary schools, elementary teachers come together in grade-level learning teams every other month to create common assessments. This horizontal articulation is a great professional learning exercise as each teacher learns from and shares with peers within the system. The second type of horizontal alignment is cross-curricular. A high school in Arkansas uses its system of goal setting to focus on literacy campuswide. All teachers in the school (including performing arts, physical education, special education, and vocational) are focused on improving student writing.

Good planning, incorporating various sources of data into goal setting, and using formative assessment techniques to monitor results will lead to more efficient and deeper levels of learning—for teachers and students.

Moving From Intention to Action

The five guidelines provide clarity of the system's current state, a necessary but not sufficient condition for system improvement. Once we understand the current system, we need to bring it into an acceptable level of stability so that the appropriate strategies can be implemented, measured, and improved.

Schools are complex, dynamic systems. At some level, the complexity is a good thing. It brings richness and synergy to the school culture—a healthy interdependence among the various parts, which manifest themselves as: multiple, interrelated processes; dynamic human relationships; and myriad tasks that combine to create a stimulating learning community. However, too much of a good thing can sometimes lead to unhealthy outcomes. If we don't understand either the complex nature of or the dynamics associated with the relationships, we run the risk of overloading the system to the point of being inefficient, ineffective, or just plain frozen in terms of its ability to perform.

It would be so much easier if we could just take the school apart, examine the pieces, fix what's wrong, and then put it back together again. But we know that approach won't work, even though there are plenty of reform strategies that appear to want to do so, either through programmatic or formulaic panaceas. There are also plenty of theories about the characteristics that cause schools to be either high performing or low performing, many of which are backed by substantial and valid research (Marzano, 2003; Ragland, Asera, & Johnson, 1999; Reeves, 2000). Unfortunately, the *characteristics* of these high- or low-performing organizations are just that—characteristics, not a system or methodology for improvement. In worthy pursuits to understand and re-create these characteristics, leaders of school improvement miss a deeper underlying opportunity to address the unhealthy complexity that actually results from fixing the system one characteristic at a time. A better approach would be to intentionally select specific actions based on the nature and causes of the problem or gap that is being resolved.

Levels of Fix

It is useful to think about improvement strategies in terms of various levels of intent and action. If we can agree on the desired outcome, then the level and type of intervention we select will have a better chance of leading to that outcome. We refer to the different types of intervention as *levels of fix*. There are three levels, each with a distinct purpose.

1. Level I: Fix the problem.
2. Level II: Improve the process.
3. Level III: Redesign the system.

To illustrate the different levels of fix, imagine a weedy flower bed or a stack of papers that never seems to go away. In both cases, there is an observable problem or opportunity for improvement. Certainly, it would be prudent to address and eliminate the problem as quickly as possible. In the case of the weedy flower bed, weed the garden; in the case of the stack of papers, file them or throw them away. There, problem solved! That is a level I fix.

Unless you have some sort of magic touch, the weeds will return and so will the papers. Why? Because there are processes and systems in place that pretty much guarantee their return. In the case of the weedy flower bed, it may be that pulling the weed, mowing it down, or clearing the bed (all level I fixes) actually serve to propagate the spread of the weed. In the case of the stack of papers, it is likely that the paper mover has a habitual pattern that generates the piles over and over again.

Applying a level II fix to either of these problems will require a deeper look into the processes that created the problem in the first place. If we isolate, define, and measure the processes that led to the results we are seeing, we will have a better chance of influencing the associated outcomes in the future. In our current examples, the processes may be endemic as in the case of the weedy garden, or they may be idiosyncratic as in the case of the piles. In either situation, it is possible to understand and influence the process using a specific and targeted approach.

However, even if the process is changed or improved, if we don't address the root cause of the problem and the underlying structures that define the system, a new or improved process is likely to result in a similar or equally annoying problem in the future. There will always be weeds, but understanding their root system and how the weeds become established can go a long way toward keeping them from getting out of control. The use of land-preparation techniques, weed-prevention products, ground cover, or mulch are all level III strategies that will serve to prevent and suppress the spread of even the hardiest of weeds. The recurring piles of paper may actually be the more difficult of the two examples to fix. In this case, a level III system intervention could include bringing in a specialist in organizational techniques, purchasing a set of filing cabinets, switching to computer-based accounting methods, or obtaining psychotherapy for the paper-piling culprit.

Improvement is as much a mindset as it is a set of tools or methods. Before an organization can take the first step, it must recognize the situation and admit that a problem or an opportunity for improvement exists. Then, examining the possibilities at many different levels can help organizational leaders become clear about what the problem really is and how broad or deep the impact of the problem might be. If we think about improvement at only a surface level, our tendency will be to create solutions that are not much more than Band-Aids. If the problem truly is a scratch or a scrape, a Band-Aid will suffice. On the other hand, if the problem is chronic, pervasive, or systemic, the solution needs to be comprehensive. A Band-Aid approach simply won't do.

Once we understand the nature of the problem, then the levels and types of strategies that can be used to address it become progressively deeper and produce results that are more enduring. At level I, we can expect to see some fairly immediate results because the problem is either resolved or redirected. Examples of level I fixes aimed at behavioral problems include adding a supervisor to the playground, issuing hall passes, or giving detentions. Level I fixes aimed at academic problems might include increasing tutorial time, serving students breakfast on test day, teaching test-taking skills, or increasing time on task.

At level II, it might take longer to see the results, but the benefits will be longer lasting and broader in scope. Level II process fixes might include the implementation of new assessment processes, the introduction of new instructional programs or methodologies, or changes in textbooks, computer programs, or daily schedules.

Finally, level III system changes might include philosophical shifts in areas that include data-informed improvement planning, pedagogy, curriculum, and assessment practices. Other level III changes might take the form of:

- Adjustments to policies (for example, accountability, employment, and governance)

- Altered attitudes and beliefs (for example, beliefs about how children learn or the role of adult learning as it pertains to student performance)

- New organizational structures (for example, professional learning communities) and infrastructures (for example, RTI supports)

- Different resource allocations (for example, time, money, information, and technology)

- New or altered relationships (for example, teacher leaders, parent involvement, and the use of instructional coaches)

To further complicate systemic improvement, what may start out as a level I or level II analysis could lead to the need for a level III improvement that almost always requires the involvement of different, if not additional, people. An example of this phenomenon was seen in a middle school science department that looked at students' performance in science on the state test. The department's level I work included an item analysis of student responses on the earth science strand. The science test was given to seventh graders in April. However, the earth science module wasn't taught until the first semester of eighth grade. This seems like a simple adjustment to make—teach earth science earlier in the middle school curriculum (level II). But curriculum is a system unto itself, which means that if this one change is made, effects are likely to ripple through the rest of the middle school curriculum and perhaps through the high school curriculum as well. Many districts have multiyear cycles for curriculum evaluation and improvement. The cycle for a particular content area may span seven years. The level III improvement would be to change the cycle of curriculum evaluation and improvement from one based on an arbitrary sequence to one based on the district's greatest areas of need.

Asking the Right Questions

Asking good questions is one part science and one part art. In the case of selecting which level of fix to pursue, it helps to think about the breadth and depth of what the data are telling you about the problem. Data that suggest that the problem is chronic or the need for impact is systemic will direct you to level III, whereas data that point to a need for urgency may move your attention to level I. Process improvements (level II) can often be found in improvement plans that span a couple of years, when the data suggest a lack of consistency of approach or a need for greater efficiency.

Once you know the level of fix on which to focus, the art of questioning starts with being tuned in to what you really want to know. Formulation of the questions will likely be driven by a theory of what you think is occurring. As you pursue the answers to your questions, your theory may not be validated, in which case, additional questions may arise. Ultimately, the process of asking good questions in pursuit of greater understanding will provide guidance to the selection of the most appropriate actions to be taken, regardless of the level of fix.

The sample questions in the following sections illustrate how the need for improvement in student performance can lead to intentional actions. There are four types of questions we should ask at each of the three levels of fix:

1. Analysis

2. Alignment

3. Improvement

4. Action

Questions for Level I

The *analysis* questions at level I—understanding and fixing the problem at the surface—are:

- What percentage of our students have mastered any given standard?
- On which standards are our students scoring at the proficient level or above?
- On which test items did we show a strong or weak performance?
- What achievement trends are we seeing over time?

Answering these questions will provide a basic understanding of overall student performance on any given measure. The bigger the test—for example, international measures and state or provincial standardized achievement tests—the more superficial the understanding.

The *alignment* questions at level I are:

- Are we teaching what we're testing?
- Are we testing what we're teaching?

In other words, what might be a simple explanation of the phenomenon that we are seeing in our level I analysis of the data? For example, a second-grade teacher team did an item analysis of their students' performance on the state test and discovered that the students were required to be able to identify a "root word" on the language arts portion of the test. The school's curriculum taught the concept of root word but used the term *base word* instead.

The *improvement* questions at level I are:

- How can we close the gap between what is being taught and what is being tested?

- How can we close the gap between what is being taught and what is being learned?

Improvement actions suggest the need for some kind of adjustment in curriculum, assessment, instruction, or all three. The important concept in this example is the relationship between a word's base and its broader use within the context of a sentence. It really doesn't matter whether we call it a *root word* or *base word* as long as students understand the structures of words and their applications. Since the measure being used is a standardized test, adjusting the assessment is not an option. This situation implies the need for adjusting instruction.

The *action* question for level I is:

- What will it take to fix the problem?

As a result of conducting the item analysis and determining the instructional misalignment with the test, the teachers adjusted their teaching of the concept so that students would recognize what they were being asked to demonstrate. Some might call this teaching to the test. We prefer to think of it as giving students every opportunity to show what they know. A relatively simple analysis should lead to a relatively simple, but not simplistic, solution. Too often, common actions include working harder and longer, trying another new program, tweaking instruction, and becoming more vigilant observers of scores. More effective actions would include researching and testing out new strategies aimed specifically at eliminating the problem.

Questions for Level II

The *analysis* questions at level II—understanding and improving the processes of teaching and learning—are:

- How do we know that our students are learning what we're teaching?

- To what extent are students able to demonstrate that they are learning what we want them to learn?

- Are increasing numbers of students, regardless of demographic profile, demonstrating competence on all standards of learning?

- Is the achievement trend we are seeing sufficient to achieve adequate yearly progress (AYP) and other targets of learning established by the district, state, province, or federal government?

These analysis questions are all about the impact of our work and the extent to which we are achieving sufficient gains. By linking performance data directly to the standards, we can derive evidence that what we are doing is making a difference in terms of student learning. Without that connection, we don't have the basis upon which to draw conclusions about the efficacy of our instruction. Results from disconnected measures are random pictures of the moment in time that students took the test. It's pretty hard to make meaningful improvements on random events—unless the improvements lead to coherent processes for connecting curriculum, assessment, and instruction.

The *alignment* questions at level II are:

- Does our curriculum align with the standards that we are expecting students to achieve?

- Are we teaching to and assessing against those standards?

A critical analysis of the state or provincial test results may show that students are being tested on standards they have not been taught, in which case, it's pretty clear that there is a process in need of improvement. Vertical and horizontal alignment of the curriculum brings coherence to the teaching process. Alignment of the curriculum with assessment brings coherence to the learning process. When either type of alignment is missing, high levels of performance can be attributed to luck or really savvy kids.

By asking the alignment questions at this level, teachers can also unearth strategies they may not have pursued. For example, a fourth-grade team discovered that students were struggling with drawing conclusions from written text on the reading portion of their state test. When the team examined the curriculum, they discovered that drawing conclusions was officially part of the fourth-grade curriculum but that teachers were not teaching it directly. Why? None of the teachers knew how to teach drawing conclusions. The team recognized this as a critical professional development opportunity that would not have surfaced had they not engaged in this level of inquiry.

The *improvement* questions at level II are:

- How can we improve our ability to connect what we expect kids to know and be able to do with what and how we teach?

- How can we be better at knowing how well our students are learning and meeting the standards?

Far too often, the gaps that exist between one grade and the next or between one related subject and the next go undetected because there is no process for examining what is taught. Even more likely, there is not a common process for assessing students' learning in an ongoing way to determine how well or if they are meeting the standards. For a process improvement to occur, there needs to be a process in place. So, the first order of business is to develop curriculum, instruction, and assessment processes that will give some measure of stability when attempting to make improvements.

The *action* question at level II is:

- What processes need to be implemented or improved so that student learning improves?

Examples of what will be needed to fix the problem at this level include: job-embedded, goal-driven professional development that facilitates dialogue for the purpose of developing and aligning curriculum; the development and use of common formative assessments; sharing and studying instructional best practices; and an analysis of data for instructional improvement.

Questions for Level III

The *analysis* questions at level III—understanding and improving the systems for teaching and learning—are:

- To what extent and at what pace are we achieving our goals?

- What systems are in place to support ongoing improvement of student learning throughout our school and district?

Level III is where the analysis of data leads to intentional, goal-driven actions. The focus of the question changes from What is? to What is possible? The data analyses that we conduct give us clues about the health of our systems and whether they support the teaching and learning process.

Data and causal analyses at this level provide us with predictive capacity and systemic solutions that can fundamentally change the patterns of results we see over time.

The *alignment* questions at level III are:

- Do our strategic goals align with our school improvement goals?
- Do policies, resource allocations, programs, and professional development support the achievement of our goals?
- Is our educational delivery system (curriculum, assessment, and instruction) aligned with our strategic intent to continuously improve student learning?

Level III alignment is the most comprehensive and the most difficult type of improvement. Because of the tremendous complexity of educational systems and the interdependent nature of the people and the work, improvements at this level require a much deeper understanding and a more strategic approach when compared with the other two levels. The tools, methods, and analyses used to create alignment at this level are similar to those used at other levels except that they require a longer-term view, greater patience, and systemwide collaboration—none of which is indigenous to the traditional education environment.

The *improvement* questions at level III are:

- How can we integrate and enhance our core educational delivery system to achieve and sustain high levels of student learning?
- What significant barriers can we remove from our schools and classrooms so that teachers are empowered to make transformational instructional changes on behalf of student learning?

The way in which we manage weeds in our garden could lead to more widespread and tenacious weed growth. Similarly, the *solutions* we put in place to manage our achievement gaps could lead to the proliferation of confusion in the system at large. Simply adding solutions to the mix is not likely to lead to better results. On the other hand, removing barriers, preventing the conditions that fuel random variation, and creating support systems and structures that engage those working inside the system will result in more powerful and sustainable improvements.

The *action* question at level III is:

- What system improvement efforts will give us the greatest leverage for overall improvement of student learning?

Problems at the deep systemic level will require solutions that include new learning and coaching and the development of widespread leadership capacity throughout the organization. Guided by goal setting and ongoing monitoring of progress, the systems approach to change necessitates continuous improvement of all aspects of the organization and classroom teaching and learning.

Level III changes have implications for every aspect of decision making, planning, and improving throughout the organization. District leaders should standardize the system and customize delivery. What does that mean? It means that from the perspective of the whole district, certain predictable and reliable systems need to be in place so that improvement work can occur with integrity at the point of delivery. Differentiated instruction, common assessments, and school improvement and RTI plans cannot be delivered with integrity if there is not a common set of core standards that is adhered to across the district. If there is no guaranteed, viable, and coherent curriculum (Marzano, 2003), no system of professional learning (Eastman, 2008; Hirsh & Killion, 2008; Killion & Roy, 2009), no means for collaboration around important goals and outcomes (DuFour & Eaker, 1998; O'Neill, Conzemius, Commodore, & Pulsfus, 2006), and no system of common formative assessments that provide ongoing data (Stiggins, Arter, Chappuis, & Chappuis, 2007), then attempts at improvement will be ineffectual; there can be no sustainable improvement of outcomes because the system within which the important work of teaching and learning occurs is unstable, unpredictable, and misguided. Thus, level III work is about designing deep, systemic improvements capable of producing substantially better and more consistent results.

When the System Can't Be Fixed or Improved

Might there be a level IV? If the system cannot be brought into an acceptable level of balance or performance, then something more dramatic is required. Recall the golf lesson when Rob said, "If you want to get substantially better, we're going to need to work on your whole swing. If you want to get a little bit better, I can give you some easy tips to improve your score." When improvement is more about being better at playing the whole game than it is about the score, a fundamental system improvement is required. When the current game isn't working at all, a whole new game needs to be played. There are some schools that are so deeply troubled that improvement is simply not good enough. Nor will improvement suffice when the system is taking on a completely different purpose, such as retooling for 21st century global learning.

Clayton Christensen is a Harvard Business School professor who has spent his career researching, writing, and teaching about innovation. Most recently, he, Michael Horn, and Curtis Johnson (2008) wrote what we think will be one of the most important books written about education in several decades: *Disrupting Class: How Disruptive Innovation Will Change the Way the World Learns*. The research for this book was not done in schools. It was done through the lens of innovation—disruptive innovation, to be more specific, a concept that is quite different from systemic improvement, which is what we have been promoting as a level III improvement strategy.

Disruptive innovation comes much closer to the concept of *adaptive change*, which is what Davidovich et al. (2010) assert will be needed to "achieve results unobtainable by improvement in the current operating paradigm" (p. 28). Disruptive innovation "disrupts the trajectory of change" (Christensen et al., 2008, p. 47) by changing the definition of what both quality and improvement mean. What may have been valuable improvements before the disruption are less relevant after the disruption, and new dimensions that may have been previously unimportant become highly valued.

To illustrate this notion, let's return to our earlier example of the telephone. One of the improvements to the telephone that was considered most valuable at the time was the introduction of the remote handset, which allowed the user to walk away from the base of the phone, untethered by a cord. This freedom, however, was limited to a set distance from the base. With the introduction of the cell phone, which can be used anywhere there is service, the remote handset, though still useful, is far less relevant. Now that this dimension is a reality, just try to take it away.

Christensen and his coauthors (2008) do an excellent job of demonstrating that public schools in America have always been about adapting to change and engaging in improvement. They cite numerous examples to illustrate the successes of our system and the difficult environments within which change has had to occur. But no one would ever have been able to predict how dramatically and quickly changes in the world economy, emerging technologies, and scientific discoveries would render our traditional models and institutions obsolete.

The authors provide a compelling case for the need to shift from the practice of "monolithic instruction of batches of students toward a modular, student-centric approach" (Christensen et al., 2008, p. 12):

> If the goal is to educate every student—asking schools to ensure that all students have the skills and capabilities to escape the chains of poverty and have an all-American shot at realizing their dreams— we must find a way to move toward a "student-centric" model. (Christensen et al., 2008, p. 38)

The authors are looking to disrupt class—not just the classroom, but social class injustices. How better to do so than via the educational process? The shift they promote is massive. It challenges everything we currently do, the technologies we use, the way we structure our classrooms, schedules, lessons, the role of teachers and teaching, the role of students and learning, and the list goes on. We encourage every educator to think boldly and to be open to where Christensen and his colleagues believe we can go. It is an opportune time to try innovation, not as a school improvement strategy, but as a social justice strategy.

Throughout this chapter, we have explored various levels and types of improvement that are available to educational leaders. Inherent in these strategies is the belief that people working together toward a common aim can and will make the changes that are needed to achieve their goals. This also assumes that goals have been set and are being pursued within a collaborative process designed for improvement. When we take the time and effort to understand the structures and dynamics of the systems within which we work, our change efforts can lead to dramatically improved results. Going forward, the challenge for educators will be to determine whether improvements to the current system are sufficient to meet the changing needs and expectations of our society and our world. If not, a different form of change may be required—adaptive or disruptive. The form schooling takes may look and feel very different, but the fundamental purpose of school will continue to be student learning. The concepts, tools, and methods for continuous improvement will always be relevant regardless of the nature or extent of the change we seek. If we can stay focused on our goals and commit to remaining true to our mission, we won't have to do it all. We will just have to do the right things well.

CHAPTER 2

Less Is More

What you focus on expands.

—CORA WHITTINGTON

In our search for the originator of the quotation "what you focus on expands," it became apparent that the message crosses many different realms and genres. From the spiritual realm to the business world to personal psychology, the idea that focus spawns growth and meaning is ubiquitous. But how does this idea work in the life of a busy teacher, school principal, or central office leader?

The concept is pretty simple. What you give your time, energy, and attention to will grow. Put another way, energy flows where attention goes. The underlying challenge for educators is finding the right thing to focus on amidst an endless stream of worthy options. For too many, the trap of busyness creates a barrier to thoughtful focus, resulting in a continuous cycle of work for the sake of getting things done. People can usually remember all the things they did during a day or week, but they can't always articulate what they accomplished. Peter Drucker, writer and management consultant, once said, "Taking action without thinking is the cause of every failure" (as cited in Shrawder, 2006, p. 4). Even if an action doesn't result in a failure, all those *things* that were completed may have precluded opportunities to do the few things that would have allowed the doer to pursue a better direction.

Resisting Initiativitis

There is an epidemic afflicting education. We call it *initiativitis*. The symptoms are observable—people frantically moving about, faces tense with concern, hands being wrung in anxious anticipation of the next thing to do, and offices strewn with piles of unfinished business. Meetings start late, cell phones ring and buzz, and eventually someone drops from sheer exhaustion.

Confusion, overload, and incoherence typify the plight of educators these days, and we are so caught up in it that we've come to believe that it's normal. Our remedy for the inflamed condition is to do more of something, anything that seems like it might work, rather than to do less with what's best. We are fooling ourselves if we believe that this frantic pace can continue and that performance will improve.

Initiativitis evolves through a series of events that occur throughout the system:

- Whenever there is a new or revised federal legislative decree, school districts are inundated with administrative rules, mandates, programs, and technical advisers, all created to "help" the districts comply. In the name of accountability, the state or province might also throw in a few of its own additional requirements, some of which are unfunded mandates placing additional stress on school and district budgets.

- In turn, the district bombards its school sites with one initiative after the next, heaping "helpful" resources like layers of blankets onto the "schools in need" until they just can't move under the weight of it all.

- The school principal, whose spinning plates are already too full, wakes up to hear her school and its teachers being maligned by the morning talk show host who is demanding that something be done!

- In the name of empowerment and capacity building, the principal downloads her to-do list to a few loyal but unsuspecting teacher leaders who already are coming in early, staying late, and are barely able to find time in their day to visit the restroom. (Conzemius, 2010, pp. 32–33)

In an attempt to eradicate the epidemic, policymakers have unwittingly exacerbated the problem by passing a series of reform programs aimed at diagnosing and treating current educational practices. One could argue about the motives behind these programs but, regardless, most of the strategies have been consistently ineffective. The sense of urgency caused by looming deadlines, ominous sanctions, and increasingly challenging targets generates a great deal of activity, all too frequently without commensurate payoff in terms of measurable results. For example, according to the Education Trust (2010), after fourteen years (1996–2010), there was a 45 percent increase in the number of fourth graders scoring proficient or above in basic math. That's slightly more than 3 percent improvement per year. Though certainly cause for some celebration, it is hardly a victory considering the starting point was 75 percent nonproficient. That leaves 30 percent of our fourth graders abysmally below the standard. Worse yet, the gaps separating achievement of African American and Latino twelfth graders from their white peers is actually larger than it was in the late 1980s. Not surprisingly, the difference in the graduation rates between African American and Latino youth compared to their white peers is also widening (Education Trust, 2010).

What began as a prescribed regimen to treat the symptoms has spawned a more pervasive problem with no long-term benefits to show for our efforts:

> In theory, mandating reform could work at one level. But theory and legislation don't cause deep, systemic and fundamental change. Legislation may ignite change in behavior in the short term but like any externally generated directive that uses fear as its motivational technique, substantive and sustainable change is unlikely. A more likely result is that the system will find a way to adjust itself to alleviate the tension rather than change itself to comply with the mandate. Furthermore, if there isn't a process that engages people in owning the change at a deep, personal level, any short-term results that may be attributed to the mandate are quickly wiped away when the source of fear is removed. (Conzemius, 2010, p. 34)

The frenetic approach and short-term thinking that are by-products of compliance-driven reform cannot be sustained and should not be sustained. We need to examine with fierce honesty the impacts that these mandates have had on our schools, not just on the test scores, but on the people—principals, teachers, students, and parents.

But change unto itself isn't really the objective. Every educator will tell you that change is happening all around. It's not just legislation that fuels the chaos. There's plenty of evidence that we add to our own burden, if not intentionally then by the absence of a more strategic approach. The prevailing practices of reform in education are more likely to mask the symptoms than to promote a cure. They include but are not limited to:

- A plethora of rapid-fire initiatives that are based on the latest and greatest idea or newest product on the market

- Short-term thinking that is not connected to nor supported by strategic intent

- One-size-fits-all events and random acts of professional development

- A narrow focus on getting off an accountability list or on a commendation list

- Curricular fixes that bring new programs and content without new context or focus

- Instructional panaceas, such as our personal favorite, "No Laptop Left Behind"

What is the impact of the explosion of initiatives on educational practice? Are we really getting healthier, or are these merely analgesic remedies that mask the real problem and ultimately generate yet more initiatives? What data do we have that indicate that our current reforms lead to better teaching and more relevant learning? How do schools and districts know whether what they are doing in the name of reform is actually producing better results, not just for a few, but overall? What needs to happen so that teachers and principals can concentrate on creating high-quality learning experiences for their students? The answers to these questions can be found in changing our habits, not changing our programs. The only cure for a disease like initiativitis is to slow down, reflect, and focus on high-leverage goals and actions that will have the greatest impact on improving results.

Cultivating New Habits

Slowing down in the midst of panic is counterintuitive. It's like expecting a gazelle to stop running in the midst of the chase. Most wouldn't recommend it. Our current sense of urgency in education is an important reminder that we're doing extremely important work, which is all the more reason why going slow to go fast is the best approach. If we continue to move at 100 miles per hour, we will miss critical steps and important opportunities to influence the outcomes of our efforts. When we slow down, we are better able to think, to create, to focus, and to act with intention as opposed to grasping at every life preserver that is thrown our way.

Educational theorists, researchers, and practitioners have long held *reflective practice* as essential for high-quality, focused learning. Indeed, deep and sustainable learning requires reflection; it may be the distinguishing characteristic that separates the learned from the learner. In their book *Reflective*

Practice to Improve Schools, Jennifer York-Barr, William A. Sommers, Gail S. Ghere, and Jo Montie (2006) trace the historical references to reflective thinking as far back as the early philosophical works of thinkers such as Buddha and Socrates. In educational literature, John Dewey is a significant contributor to the foundational concepts of reflective practice. His definition of *reflective thinking* is remarkably similar to what we now refer to as *action research*: "a systematic, scientific process of describing experience, articulating questions that arise from experience, generating hypotheses which include considering sources outside oneself, and taking intelligent action to test hypotheses" (York-Barr et al., 2006, p. 5).

Modern literature is replete with references to and support for teachers as reflective practitioners. Karen F. Osterman and Robert B. Kottkamp (2004) define *reflective practice* much the same way that Dewey did with an additional emphasis on gathering and analyzing data as a "keystone of reflective practice" (York-Barr et al., 2006, p. 7). Max van Manen (2002) distinguishes forms of reflective thinking based on the unique purpose each serves. The purpose of *technical reflection* is to examine the strategies, methods, and skills used to achieve a predetermined goal. In this type of reflection, the individual or team seeks to determine whether the strategies applied were effective in moving toward or accomplishing the goal. *Practical reflection* takes into account the assumptions underlying the methods selected to achieve the goal, including whether the goal itself was appropriate.

Art Costa (2006) makes a sound case for everyone in the school engaging in reflective learning, called *habitual reflection*, which means that it becomes embedded in the organization's culture. To embed it in the culture, leaders need to establish systemwide processes for reflection, assure time for individuals and teams to engage in reflection, and commit to exploring a new set of assumptions about what constitutes real and deep learning.

Costa (2006) asserts that the traditional habits of educators and current assumptions about learning are antithetical to habitual reflection:

> We are trained to believe that deep learning means knowing accepted truths rather than developing capacities for effective and thoughtful action; acquiring knowledge is for passing tests rather than accumulating wisdom and personal meaning. We are taught to value certainty rather than doubt, to give quick answers rather than to inquire, and to know which choice is correct rather than to reflect on alternatives. (p. xv)

Costa (2006) goes on to state that the extent to which the adults in our schools engage in reflective practices will have a direct and noticeable effect on the reflective behaviors of the young people in our schools: "Because imitation is the most basic form of learning, impressionable students often need to see adults reflect on their practice. Adults are not only facilitators of meaning making but also models of reflection" (p. xviii). It is the role of the adults in the system—teachers, parents, aides, support staff, and administrators—to help students approach their learning in thoughtful and strategic ways. With the guidance and support of their teachers, students can learn to assess and monitor their progress during the learning experience, to "construct meaning from the content learned as well as from the process of learning it," and to modify their actions and apply what they have learned to other contexts and settings (York-Barr et al., 2006, p. xviii).

But where is the opportunity for such work during the day? Our busy classrooms are overburdened with too many tasks and not enough time, making reflection almost impossible. Perhaps the old adage that less is more applies:

- Less content, more depth

- Less reacting, more planning

- Less fact-finding, more discovery

- Less about the test, more about the learning

It can all be summed up as fewer priorities, better results.

Setting High-Priority Goals

When we talk about reflection, we are referring not only to the practice of taking time to examine what we are doing and how we are doing it but also taking the time to make meaning of the data that reflect the efficacy of our actions. Using data to focus our efforts on high-priority outcomes ultimately links reflective practice to goal-oriented action. By reflecting on data within the context of goal setting, principals, teachers, and students are able to monitor their progress and make better decisions about teaching and learning.

We use the SMART acronym (strategic and specific, measurable, attainable, results oriented, and time bound) to define the criteria for setting data-informed, high-priority goals. The SMART acronym, as it applies to goal setting, has been used in business for decades, and now SMART goals are showing up everywhere in the educational enterprise. District strategic plans, school improvement plans, and even grade-, department-, and team-level plans include SMART goals.

SMART goals are based on the organization's greatest area of need, which in turn is based on the Pareto principle, a statistical concept from the quality movement that brings focus to the goal-setting process by eliminating the need to solve every problem one by one. The Pareto principle is based on the fact that within any system, there are a few causes that account for the majority of the problems. It is often referred to as the 80/20 rule because most of the problems (80 percent) can be eliminated if we focus on the vital few (20 percent) causes. In the case of goal setting, the Pareto principle gives us permission to isolate a few, high-leverage priorities and seek to resolve those, knowing that everything else will benefit from our improvement efforts. By focusing on only the vital few needs, greater gains can be achieved not only in the goal area but also in other parts of the system that are affected by the achievement of the goal. So, if we attend to the vital few things that will have the greatest impact, a whole system of problems can be addressed simultaneously, allowing us to maximize the efficient use of our time and resources. Nothing can dilute focus faster than having too many goals.

When writing a SMART goal, keep in mind that the goal should address the GAN at the appropriate altitude (district, school, team, or student). Altitude is important because the type of measure that is used will change depending on the level of analysis. For example, at the district and school levels, the GAN is established using an annual summative measure. As the analysis moves to the team and classroom levels, benchmark and common formative measures are more appropriate. For individual students, GAN is established based on specific standards, skills, or knowledge gaps that have been identified on actual performance measures, teacher-made assessments, and diagnostic instruments. The example that follows is a school-level GAN analysis. It provides a starting point for setting the school's SMART goal.

An approach that is specifically designed to identify a school's GAN and build commitment to and understanding of the resulting priorities that are identified involves the analysis of three gaps:

1. The accountability gap—The difference between where we are today and where we will be held accountable at some point in the future

2. The proficiency gap—The difference between where we are today and 100 percent of our children being proficient by some set of standards as measured by an agreed-upon assessment

3. The change-over-time gap—The difference between our baseline performance data and where we are today in terms of student proficiency

The importance of knowing the accountability gap is fairly obvious. That is the gap that is driven by some district, state, provincial, or federal requirement and is usually accompanied by either a consequence for not achieving the target or some reward or celebration for attaining it. The accountability gap is a compliance measure. Table 2.1 shows how data can be used to find the accountability gap.

Table 2.1: Finding the Accountability Gap—Schoolwide Data on Standards-Based Assessment

% Meets and Exceeds (or % Proficient and Advanced)

	Reading	Writing	Math	Science	Social Studies
Accountability target	85	80	80	80	85
Most recent data	76	79	71	78	80
Accountability gap	-9	-1	-9	-2	-5

On the other hand, the proficiency gap gets to the heart of why we entered the profession in the first place. It measures the real goal, which is working toward all children succeeding. We also refer to this as the commitment gap. It challenges our spirit as much as our decisions about the work. Our desire to close the proficiency gap fuels the urgency for change. Table 2.2 provides an example of determining the proficiency gap.

Table 2.2: Finding the Proficiency Gap—Schoolwide Data on Standards-Based Assessment

% Meets and Exceeds (or % Proficient and Advanced)

	Reading	Writing	Math	Science	Social Studies
Proficiency target	100	100	100	100	100
Most recent data	76	79	71	78	80
Proficiency gap	-24	-21	-29	-22	-20

The third gap, change over time, provides a better picture of what our existing practices (for example, curriculum, assessment, and instruction) are producing and gives us some sense of what we might predict in the future. If the trend looks good, damn the torpedoes, full speed ahead! If the trend is headed south or if there is no trend (that is, random variation or flatlined performance), transform the system since it's either going in the wrong direction, going out of control, or going nowhere. Table 2.3 shows the calculation of change over time.

Table 2.3: Finding the Change-Over-Time Gap—Schoolwide Data on Standards-Based Assessment

% Meets and Exceeds (or % Proficient and Advanced)

	Reading	Writing	Math	Science	Social Studies
Most recent data	76	79	71	78	80
Baseline data	68	72	67	72	69
Change over time	+8	+7	+4	+6	+11

Each of these gaps has a unique set of calculations associated with it, as shown in the previous tables. When combined, as shown in table 2.4 (page 50), they narrow our focus to the subject of greatest need or concern, the GAN. In this case, math is our GAN. Though the accountability gap is the same for reading and math, when we move to the proficiency gap, it becomes clear that the school's performance in math is the lowest relative to all the other subjects. The reason for this difference is in how the targets were set for the accountability gap. The accountability targets can vary from one year to the next, and they can vary across subjects. Because they are numbers that represent expectations set by a higher authority (for example, the federal government, a state or provincial agency, or a district's board of education), they also vary from place to place. Sometimes the accountability targets are based on the mean score of a larger population (for example, a state or provincial average); sometimes they are set as a computed growth target based on current performance; and sometimes they are set for political reasons. Because of this inherent variation of expectations, it is important to use a more stable proficiency target in conjunction with the accountability targets. By definition, the proficiency target is always 100 percent. Finally, in this example, when we calculate the change over time, math performance shows the smallest gain. Change over time is an important analysis for a number of reasons. First, if we only use our most recent year's scores as our means for determining GAN, we have really only identified the GAN for one year based on a snapshot of student performance. We all know that a single data point is not always the most accurate picture, and it is impossible to discern a trend

Table 2.4: Finding the School-Level Subject GAN

	Reading	Writing	Math	Science	Social Studies
Accountability gap: For the current year, what is the gap between % meets and exceeds or % proficient and advanced and the federal, state, or provincial target performance?	-9	-1	-9	-2	-5
Proficiency gap: For the current year, what is the gap between the % meets and exceeds or % proficient and advanced and 100%?	-24	-21	-29	-22	-20
Change-over-time gap: From your first year of data to present day, how much change has occurred in % meets and exceeds or % proficient and advanced?	+8	+7	+4	+6	+11

or pattern based on only one point in time. Second, the subject GAN from the most recent year may be the lowest, but if you look at data over time, you may see that there has been a steady and continuous trend upward, which means that something the school is doing is working. In that case, we'd suggest that a different subject be selected as the GAN, one that has shown no gain or even a loss of performance over time. For the change-over-time gap, it is very useful to graph the results to see the pattern of change from baseline to present day for each subject. The graphs can also illustrate relative changes across subject areas.

Once we have isolated the GAN, it is time to take a deeper look into the data to find the specific areas (for example, standards, skills, and knowledge) that represent the biggest gaps in student learning schoolwide. Here is where the Pareto principle is so valuable. By isolating the vital few areas of concern that are at the root of the problem and then closing those specific achievement gaps for individuals and subgroups of students, tremendous overall gains can be made across subjects and schoolwide.

In our example, math was the subject area of greatest need for the school. You might ask, "How can a schoolwide goal focus on a single subject if you're in a middle or high school where only the math department teaches math?" The same question will come up regardless of which subject is selected simply because many middle and high schools are structured around content-area specialties. A couple of short stories will best illustrate how an entire school is able to focus on one subject.

This question came up in a recent goal-setting workshop with a large urban high school in Texas. The staff had gone through the GAN analysis, and math was determined to be the school's focus. One brave teacher posed the question, and before we had a chance to answer, his colleague spoke up and offered a response. She said that she was using geometry formulas, concepts, and vocabulary in several of her classes at each of the grade levels. She went on to explain in some detail how what she was teaching met her curriculum standards and where she was going next with trigonometry concepts. She was the art teacher.

In another high school, this one in Ohio, the staff worked on cross-curricular vocabulary using math as the focus. All subject areas easily found math vocabulary, skills, and knowledge referred to in their content standards, curriculum, and lesson plans. The important thing to remember is that we are not asking all teachers to become proficient in teaching the GAN subject. We are asking them to reinforce schoolwide efforts and to support the schoolwide goal by emphasizing GAN-related standards in teaching their own subjects.

If it is too cumbersome or difficult to convince staff members to focus on a single-subject GAN, consider research by Reeves (2000), in which it was discovered that a common focus on a specific skill set led to broad-based improvements across all subjects. This occurred because the particular skill set that was improved wasn't subject specific—it was higher-order thinking and learning skills that could be applied in all subjects. Another key aspect was that the entire school was focused on closing the gaps. Even in schools with challenging demographic profiles, when school interventions and teaching strategies align toward the pursuit of a measurable, time-bound goal aimed at closing the most significant learning gaps, breakthrough improvements will result.

The GAN represents a large body of skill and knowledge. For the SMART goal to be *specific*, the GAN needs to be broken down into smaller, more manageable parts that represent the greatest areas of need within the subject GAN, using the Pareto principle.

We use a simple but powerful strategy called *zone analysis* to examine the data more deeply. In the case of the schoolwide goal, the data used for the zone analysis can be found in the strands, objectives, or standards of the summative test. As goal setting moves to the team, classroom, and student levels, this analysis can be done on any set of data including grades, rubrics, weekly quizzes, benchmark assessments, and the like. The zone analysis incorporates the use of a color-coding system to identify the specific skills or standards that are contributing to the largest achievement gaps. The color coding also provides a visual representation of the subpopulations of students who are struggling in the school's GAN.

The zone analysis is meant to differentiate the levels of proficiency within a particular skill set or standard by disaggregating—that is, taking apart—the data. By breaking the data into more specific zones of performance, it becomes easier to see where the focus for improvement needs to be. Without this kind of analysis, all student performance remains lumped into an average, which tells us little about individual student performance and provides almost no guidance on what to do about it.

The first step in conducting a zone analysis is to create a conversion chart like the one shown in table 2.5 that establishes the cut scores for the particular measures or assessments that are being used. This chart converts scores or percentages into colors. The purpose of the conversion chart is to help us detect ranges of performance. The cut scores are not proficiency standards or goals. They are selected based on the existing data with an eye toward assuring that there is an appropriate spread of performance across all color zones.

Table 2.5: Conversion Chart

	ACT Composite	% Meets or Exceeds	% Correct	Rubric (6 Points)
Green zone	25+	90–100	85–100	5–6
Blue zone	20–24	77–89	70–84	4
Yellow zone	17–19	61–76	51–69	3
Red zone	<17	<61	<51	1–2

Once the conversion chart has been agreed upon, the next step is to use the chart to color-code the data. For the purposes of writing a school-level goal, the entire faculty, working in cross-curricular or mixed grade-level teams look at levels of proficiency earned by all students on the strands of an annual summative measure. They use the information labeled *% proficient and advanced* or *% meets and exceeds* to determine which standards to focus on for improvement. This analysis reveals the relative areas of need and ultimately leads to the identification of specific students and specific skill sets that require the attention of the school.

There is no limit to the ways in which the zone analysis process can be applied. The key to its usefulness is that it helps focus interventions based on student learning needs. That can be extremely useful when it comes to differentiating instruction, informing RTI plans, grouping students for remediation, reteaching, and enrichment.

Getting From GAN to Goal

Determining the GAN and then utilizing zone analysis leads directly to the development of focused, high-priority goals and strategies that affect and improve the entire system at every level. The biggest challenges when creating a SMART goal are making sure that all of the criteria are met and that the goal can be monitored over time as improvements are implemented and studied. Collaborative goal writing is further complicated by the different styles and skills of the participants. We developed the SMART Goal Tree Diagram as a tool to help minimize conflicts and confusion when creating the goal in such situations. Use of the goal tree keeps the team focused and simplifies the decision making around what to include. It is designed to ensure that all aspects of SMART are present when the goal writing is complete.

To illustrate, let's look at a typical goal and see how we can make it SMARTer using the SMART Goal Tree Diagram. Let's say that the school has identified literacy as its GAN and that it has set the following goal to guide its school improvement plan: "To implement a balanced literacy program in our school."

The first distinction that needs to be made is the difference between a *process* goal and a *results* goal. The example is a process goal. It describes what the school wants to do but not what the school is hoping to accomplish by doing so. To clarify, it is useful to ask the question, What will we have when we are done? In this case, we will have a balanced literacy program, which is a good thing, but we won't know anything about how student learning has improved. The focus of this improvement goal is programmatic, not student learning. The goal can be extended by adding the phrase *so that . . .*

This should help to get to the *result* in student learning terms: "We want to implement a balanced literacy program in our school so that all students are reading at grade level or above," or, " . . . so that all students become proficient readers." Note that these examples do not yet include the element of time. The school results goal that we formulate is the first element in our tree diagram, as shown in figure 2.1.

School Results Goal

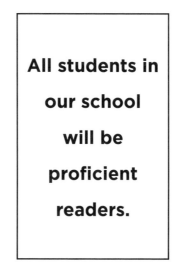

Figure 2.1: School results goal.

A SMART goal should be associated with defined indicators and measures; if not, it is akin to a powerful car with no gauges on the dashboard. The faculty must be able to operationally define what the achieved goal will look like and then find various means of measuring along the way. The indicators are the specific standards, skills, or knowledge within the goal's subject area that were identified using the zone analysis. A SMART goal should have at least one indicator and one measure but no more than three or four of each so that the goal doesn't become overwhelming. After the goal is articulated, a mind shift often occurs as the faculty defines which indicators will best close the achievement gaps and how they will measure progress toward those indicators. What existing measures can be used to inform progress? Are they the right ones? Do they measure at the appropriate altitude to support progress-monitoring decisions?

Returning to our example, reading is one aspect of literacy; it incorporates a variety of skills that translate into proficiency, not just in the subject of reading, but across all subject areas. To be more *specific* (that is, getting to the Pareto effect), the faculty looks at the strand data on the state test and other common measures of reading that are used in their school and district. By conducting the zone analysis, they discover, for use in our example, that the biggest skill gaps are in comprehension, fluency, and vocabulary development. Upon further analysis, they discover that these skills are particularly low among students of poverty. These findings become the focal points for building the indicator branches of the goal tree, as reflected in figure 2.2.

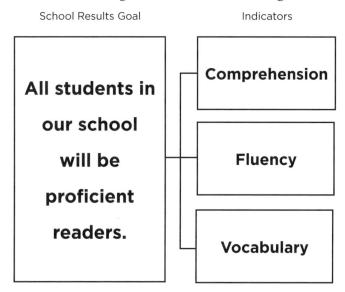

Figure 2.2: School results goal with indicators.

For each skill, there are multiple standards and ways of assessing students against those standards. Many schools now use formative measures such as the Northwest Evaluation Association's Measures of Academic Progress™ (MAP™) and AIMSweb™. Such assessments give general guidance to school-based progress monitoring, which is appropriate for school improvement planning. However, the real power of this process is revealed when common formative assessments are used in classrooms to monitor individual student performance and progress. Let's return to our goal tree in figure 2.3 (page 56) to see where *measures* fits in.

To gain and maintain momentum toward realization, a SMART goal should incorporate some way to monitor progress. Progress is not measured by completing the goal or the process; it's measured by the rate and the degree of improvement that occur when incremental targets leading to the goal are

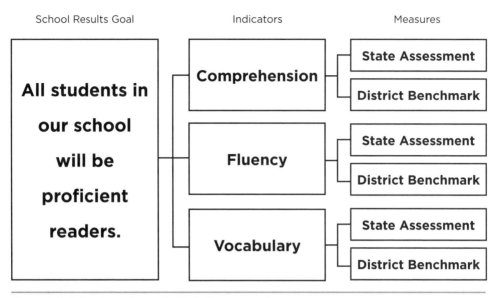

Figure 2.3: School results goal with indicators and measures.

achieved. Time and again, we've seen the improvement process come alive through ongoing and collaborative progress monitoring. Teachers begin to see the faces of their students in the data that they're required to examine. Students begin to see the pertinence of what they are learning.

So far, our example goal is *results oriented*, *strategic and specific*, and *measurable*. *Attainability* and *time* are complementary aspects of a SMART goal that are used to define targets—incremental steps toward the *results* goal. We must consider our time frame when deciding what is truly attainable. Since the targets are directly connected to the specific indicators and measures, the time frames established for reaching the targets need to reflect the frequency of the assessments and what is realistic in terms of the level of skill required for mastering the standard.

There are two ways to add time to the goal tree:

1. Include a time frame in the results box of the goal tree.

2. Specify a time limit for each improvement target since targets are intermediate increments toward the larger results goal.

With regard to state tests, the time frames are annual. When it comes to district benchmarks, the time frames will vary. The benchmarks may be administered as pre- and postassessments in fall and spring, or they may include midterm assessments.

After we add the time element, our SMART Goal Tree Diagram is complete, as shown in figure 2.4 (page 58). This visual tool and reference clarifies how the goal statement is integrally connected to standards and assessments and includes the time frame for attaining specific results.

Specific targets can also be set for subgroups. For example, if the data indicate that students of poverty and English learners performed particularly below standard on one or more of the indicators, a separate target should be set and monitored for these groups of students. These targets are attached to the branch of the tree directly related to the indicator(s) of concern.

Once the team has completed the goal tree, they should pause and reflect on the components of the goal either individually or as a team. To facilitate this reflection, we created the SMART Goal Tree Rubric to help gauge the degree to which SMART goals are fully developed, as shown in table 2.6 (page 59).

Step back and compare the usefulness of the completed goal to the initial goal statement. It is now clear which specific areas of literacy are most in need of improvement, and there is a time-referenced plan for moving toward a different end. The strategies that are put in place to achieve this goal may include adopting and implementing a balanced literacy program; however, other strategies might be included as well. The difference between selecting strategies to close specific and measurable achievement gaps and random acts of improvement is that the goal-driven strategies are selected from those that research has shown will move the school toward the goal. Strategies for closing the gaps for subgroups of students can be identified and linked to their specific targets of performance as well. As a result, these students are far less likely to fall between the proverbial cracks in the system. Strategies that are researched and selected specifically for the subgroups in greatest need should fall cleanly into the school's RTI plan.

On a final note, using SMART goals to select and monitor the effectiveness of research-based strategies should also help the school determine what's not working and what to abandon in the name of focused improvement. This is a data-driven and intentional antidote for initiativitis.

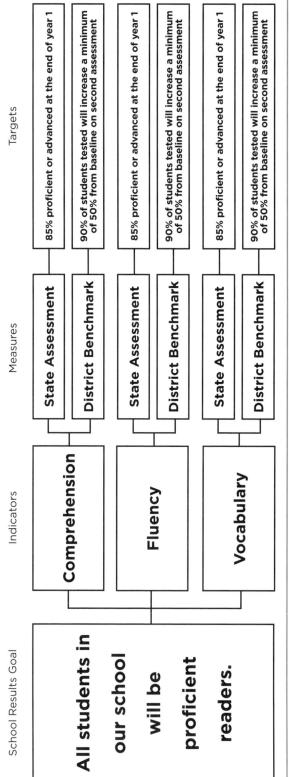

Figure 2.4: Complete school results goal in tree diagram.

Table 2.6: SMART Goal Tree Rubric

	1	2	3	4
Structure	Goal has not been translated into a tree diagram.	Goal has been translated into a tree diagram with an attempt to properly identify indicators, measures, and targets.	Goal is in a tree diagram structure with indicators, measures, and targets properly identified and aligned.	Goal is in a tree diagram structure with two to three indicators, appropriate formative and summative measures, and multiple progress targets defined and aligned.
Use of data	Goal is not based on analysis of data.	Goal, indicators, and targets are derived from an analysis of standardized test scores and focus on one GAN.	Goal, indicators, and targets are derived from an analysis of standardized test scores and local assessments. Goal focuses on one GAN. Targets are defined for subgroups.	Goal, indicators, and targets are derived from an analysis of multiple years of standardized test scores and local assessments. Goal focuses on one GAN. Targets are defined for subgroups and further defined by zones.
Time frame	Goal is not time bound.	Goal includes a specific time reference for accountability.	Goal and targets include specific time references for accountability.	Goal and targets for subgroups and zones include specific time references for accountability.
Goal setting	Goal is not formulated, or only process goal is formulated.	Results goal is formulated based on data analysis. Attainability may be questionable as too low or too high.	Results goal is formulated based on data analysis of summative measures. Attainability seems reasonable and not too easy.	Results goal is formulated based on data analysis using multiple measures. Attainability is challenging but not unreasonable.
Indicators	Standards are not identified within the goal area.	Goal is further refined by the identification of several specific standards for focus, but data have not been reviewed.	Goal is further refined by several specific standards for focus based on a review of data.	Goal is further refined by identification of no more than three specific standards that have been selected based on review of multiple years of data.
Measures	Standardized test scores are the only measure of goal progress.	Both formative and summative measures are used to assess progress on the goal.	Both formative and summative measures are used to assess progress on the goal and on the indicators.	Formative and summative measures show increasing sophistication of alignment with the specific indicators.
Monitoring	There is no evidence of monitoring.	Goal is monitored annually.	Goal and targets are monitored according to the frequency of the measures.	Goal and targets are monitored according to the frequency of the measures. Progress is visible via student movement through the zones.

CHAPTER 3

Putting SMART Goals to Work

In the absence of clearly-defined goals, we become strangely loyal to performing daily trivia until ultimately we become enslaved by it.

—Robert Heinlein

How many schools and districts incorporate or require the use of goals? We'd hazard a guess to say that the vast majority do. School improvement plans require goal writing, and strategic plans employ goals as a component part of the methodology. Superintendents are asked by their boards to set goals. Often, as part of the performance management process, individuals are asked to set goals at the beginning of the year, not to be seen again until they are reviewed during a formal year-end evaluation and then only maybe.

Much time and energy is spent writing goals, which may or may not lead to tangible results. Goals seem to appear and then disappear as if writing the goal is what it's all about. For too many schools and school systems, writing goals has become an exercise in getting the task of goal writing done and off the list. It is a natural human tendency to want to complete a task and check it off our list of things to do. The sense of completion and accomplishment is refreshing. It fortifies us to move on to the next item while serving as evidence that we have made progress. However, viewing goals as tasks to complete does little to inspire goal-related action; more often than not, goal writing represents the end of the action. Unless goals guide actions that align everyone in the system, including students, toward the desired outcome of student learning, what is the point of the goal-writing exercise?

We've heard, "We do SMART goals," over and over again. However, when we dig deeper, a different picture emerges:

- The goal statements themselves are frequently not truly SMART.

- The goal or goals may have nothing to do with the GAN.

- Goal statements are made without reference to the learning standards that should serve as indicators of what is being addressed and the appropriate vehicles for their measurement.

- Intermediate target dates that establish periodicity for measuring progress are absent.

- There are too many goals, making a lack of focus almost unavoidable.

- It is not clearly understood or articulated how fully developed SMART goals fit in the larger, ongoing process of improvement.

- District and school leaders are unsure of their role in the process.

- While goals have been articulated at the district and school levels, grade-level and curriculum teams have not been engaged in the process.

- Goals are not being used by individual students to lead their own learning and create purpose in their academic lives.

Even if a school's goals are SMART by definition, their impact will be limited if they are left to stand on their own. Having a goal is one small part of what it means to be SMART about improvement.

How do we set up conditions during the goal-setting process that will maximize success during implementation? The process begins with the dialogue and collaborative data analysis that precede formulation of the actual goal, as outlined in chapter 2. This is where priorities are defined and agreed upon and where the learning community coalesces around its common purpose. The team then clearly defines the goal and proceeds to focus on finding the most effective instructional practices and professional development that will lead to goal attainment. *This* is what should drive the selection of interventions, strategies, new programs, and instructional changes.

Focusing Systemic Leadership Roles

SMART goals exist within a context of other improvement work, including the alignment of goals throughout the learning system. It is within the realm of districts to articulate their vision with enough specificity that those who are bringing it to life have a clear direction to follow. Robert Marzano and Timothy Waters (2009) list five district-level responsibilities that are tied to the use of goals:

1. Ensuring collaborative goal setting

2. Establishing nonnegotiable goals for achievement and instruction

3. Creating board alignment with and support for district goals

4. Monitoring achievement and instruction goals

5. Allocating resources to support the goals for achievement and instruction (p. 6)

It is the responsibility of the superintendent and board to gather key stakeholders together for collaborative goal setting, building leadership capacity to sustain collective vision and focus. One of the most important stakeholder groups, if not the most important, is principals. There are a number of reasons why this position is so critical to systemwide improvement. First, the pivotal use of goals at the school level—guiding campus-level improvement while contributing to district-level, strategic priorities—requires the principal to maintain a constant presence in the larger system of goal management. This calls for a solid knowledge of what the goal management system entails and how changes in a level of goal setting and monitoring affect the whole and the flexibility to assist with needed adjustments as continuous improvement occurs.

Second, it is the principal who ensures that a district's instructional program is carried out with integrity at the school level. Principals do this by developing shared leadership for student learning among all members of their school staff, building the structures, and providing the time that allows the staff to engage in campus- and team-level conversations focused on the implementation and improvement of the instructional program. Principals need to know that their authority is supported by central office administrators, and they need opportunities to hone their own instructional leadership skills.

Principals have a third crucial role: to be the advocate and champion of goal-driven work at their sites. The following is an example of this role in action. In a district in Colorado, a middle school faculty created a singular SMART goal for their school. With assistance and encouragement from their principal, they conducted a sustained and hawk-like vigilance on their progress toward meeting the goal. Working at every grade level and in every content area, teacher learning teams created, administered, and analyzed common assessments in the goal area and shared the results with their peer leadership team for review.

They all agreed that leadership focus and perseverance were critical during this work. We asked the principal how he kept all of the separate departments in his school on the same page with regard to their schoolwide goal. He said, "It all has to do with where I put my eyes. If they see that my attention is focused on the goal and that I am looking for evidence that shows our progress toward the goal, then that's where they tend to focus as well. It's my job to make sure our goal never leaves our field of vision."

Finally, it is the role of the principal to set the stage for building a collaborative, data-rich, and goal-relevant learning environment. While accountability for goal attainment is important, even more important is how the principal establishes both the culture and the leadership capacity needed to move the entire school to achieve the goal. Building and sustaining solid, trusting relationships and knowing exactly when and how to spur people on to higher levels of commitment is an essential leadership responsibility. A school does not become a professional learning community by accident but rather through thoughtful leadership and a commitment to shared focus on student learning and professional growth within a healthy system.

Designing Effective PLCs

Professional learning communities provide the time and place for collaborative learning, instructional improvement, and goal-relevant action. A school that aspires to be a PLC takes on the work of being a community of professionals who learn through teaching and learning. Everyone knows about and learns from the work of others. At the team level, all teachers share responsibility for teaching and learning, be it within a specific content area or at a grade level. At the classroom level, the teacher and the students share responsibility for progress toward their collective learning. Finally, at the student level, every learner is able to articulate what he or she needs to learn and where his or her learning currently is in relation to that. SMART goals provide the strategic data-driven focus that assists everyone from the individual student to the teacher to the team to the school in sharing responsibility for success. As summarized by Shirley Hord and William Sommers (2008) in *Leading Professional Learning Communities*, five components of professional learning communities recur across the literature. They are:

1. Shared beliefs, values, and vision
2. Shared and supportive leadership

3. Collective learning and its application (*intentional collective learning* as subsequently used by Hord and Sommers)

4. Supportive conditions

5. Shared personal practice

These things don't just happen because they are deemed desirable. They happen first by design and then by intentional and shared leadership focused on instructional improvement (Elmore, 2000). The use of SMART goals within a process that is designed to inform instructional decision making is what leads to better results.

We asked teachers and their principals what was different about their school improvement conversations today as compared with conversations they were having five years ago. They were quick to respond with some fairly clear distinctions:

- There's much more use of data with a focus on learning, less on grading. Our conversations have more purpose and more focus, and we're questioning our current practice. Staff development is more relevant.

- Working together on one goal creates consistency in meaning and challenges us to have higher standards.

- Having a clear focus sends a strong message about priorities. That helps teachers and kids make better decisions.

Teachers also find that using SMART goals as a tool for classroom focus and decision making can be an energizing way to get students to pay attention to what's most important. One teacher shared her team's goal with her middle school mathematics class and then used classroom-based assessments to monitor progress toward the goal. Students showed great interest and pride in seeing their learning and their performance move the entire class toward their teacher's goal. They committed to help their teacher by improving their collective results.

As teachers come together to engage in important conversations, they realize that what is good for their learning is also good for their students' learning. Perhaps one of the greatest improvement opportunities afforded by PLCs is the movement toward a student-centric context, in which learning is guided by individual student goals, gauged using multiple formative measures. Therefore, we respectfully add a sixth component to PLCs:

6. Student-centric practices as a core strategy for improvement

Creating Student-Centric Classrooms

Few of us would deny that motivation is a significant factor in learning. We know from our own experience that when we are interested in a topic or see the benefit of learning a new skill, we'll spend untold hours and dollars pursuing it. Why? Perhaps because it promises to improve our overall quality of life, or maybe it's something that is intellectually stimulating, or it might be something that we've always wanted to do:

> The key to motivation is motive. It's the why. It's what gives us the energy to stay strong in hard moments. It gives the courage to recommit to the course of action we chose. It gives us the strength to say "no" because we connect with a deeper "yes!" burning inside. (Covey, 1994, p. 142)

William Damon (2008) suggests that the question of purpose provides the route to excellence: "Only when students discover personal meaning in their work do they apply their efforts with focus and imagination" (p. 10). Finding personal meaning is a function of the student's clarity about what is important and the ability of educators and parents to assist the student in connecting what's important today with what's possible tomorrow.

How many students would say that their future looks bright and that they are responsible for making their preferred future a reality? For too many, involvement with drugs and the lure of life on the streets is far more motivating and empowering than anything they might experience in school or at home. The future may be seen as predetermined or something to think about later in life.

How can educators help students find their "burning yes" for school? What do we need to do to help students see that academic excellence can get them to a better place in life when so many of the messages they receive are telling them otherwise? Discovering personal meaning shouldn't be a random act, the purview of a select few, or a function of personality. Curriculum, instruction, and assessment practices that continuously engage students in the pursuit of relevant content within the context of a larger purpose can go a long way toward pulling the reluctant learner back into the fold.

Research on the factors that significantly affect student learning provides us with clear-cut direction for bringing meaning and purpose to the classroom experience. Marzano (2003) cites several school, teacher, and student factors that affect student learning. They include but are not limited to:

- Challenging goals combined with effective feedback
- Instructional strategies
- Student motivation to learn

Responsibility for the first two is traditionally left in the hands of the teachers—setting goals *for* students and selecting instructional strategies that promote the content knowledge *educators* have determined to be most appropriate. Engaging students in setting their own goals with consistent feedback about their progress while empowering them to judge the way something is being taught allows students to own their learning. This is incredibly motivating to students. They realize that with effort they can learn and succeed in school.

Margaret Wang, Geneva Haertel, and Herbert Walberg (1993) conducted a meta-analysis of more than 11,000 factors and discovered that active participation in the learning process and student engagement in setting and monitoring their own goals were the top two influencers of success. Paul Black and Dylan Wiliam (1998) conducted a similar study and discovered that when students are involved, "formative assessments produce significant and often substantial learning gains" (p. 140). Formative assessments are not simply ongoing assessment events that help teachers plan. In their truest form, students are actively involved in learning about their own performance alongside their teachers. It is not just important that we conduct formative assessments. The power lies in how we do the assessments and how we use the resulting information to inform learning overall, that is, as an engaging learning opportunity for students.

The best way to bring focus and meaning to learning is to get students involved in directing and monitoring their own progress. That means that students will be responsible for:

- Discovering their individual GAN
- Setting their own SMART goals
- Monitoring their own progress
- Working with their teachers, parents, and peers to devise strategies that work for them

Putting students in charge of their learning will have positive compounding effects over the years, resulting in an increasing sense of self-efficacy and personal meaning.

The student SMART goals process assumes that students will not only set and monitor their own learning goals and targets, but that they will engage in collaborative practices with their peers to select, try out, and assess new learning strategies for achieving their goals. The focus of the student SMART goals process is the individual learner in relation to what he or she is expected to learn. When every learner knows and is able to operate from this place, there is greater flexibility for grouping, peer assistance, and pacing within communities of learning, supporting 21st century skills that require collaboration, communication, critical thinking, and creativity. Implicit in the establishment of classroom-based learning communities is the belief that when students work cooperatively to achieve common goals, the result will be higher levels of learning, more satisfying experiences, and shared responsibility for the success of all. Student learning communities mirror the structure and process of professional learning communities.

Students learning in community is not a new idea. Educators, authors, researchers, and policymakers have been exploring a variety of cooperative learning venues and practices for decades. If you google *cooperative learning*, you'll find 4.2 million references, including practices that reach as far back as the late 1800s in both business and education.

Research in this area compares the impact of cooperative, competitive, and individual efforts on student outcomes, and it classifies the results in three areas: (1) achievement, (2) relationships, and (3) psychological health (Johnson & Johnson, 1989). Competitive classroom environments create negative interdependence among students as they set and seek to achieve their goals. Students must, by virtue of the competitive context, work against one another; they can only achieve their goals if others do not (Deutsch, 1962; Johnson & Johnson, 1989). Most contemporary classrooms are not intentionally designed to be competitive environments, but many of our grading, testing, and instructional practices evoke implicit messages that encourage individualistic, if not competitive, aspirations and behaviors. Even the subtle ways in which teachers praise or recognize individual accomplishments can be construed to mean that cooperation and collaboration are less valued approaches for learning.

What have we learned from nearly six hundred experimental and more than one hundred correlation studies conducted over 110 years? We've learned that in order to do well in school, students need to feel that they are accepted and belong, have positive learning relationships with their peers and teachers, and believe that they can be successful in the academic and social configuration of school. When students know that with effort they can learn, even if they're struggling, schools produce individuals who know that they have ability and competence.

There are many ways to think about students' academic interactions with their peers. Cooperative learning groups, the instructional use of small groups working together to advance learning, is one example. Peer tutors, peer mentors, learning partners, problem-solving teams, project teams, and adventure-based learning all have merit based on the specific purposes they serve. The important question is not which one is best, but what will students need to be successful learners regardless of the collaborative strategies employed?

Simply seating students in clusters or teams will not necessarily result in cooperative learning. That is not true for adults, so why would we think it would work for our students? Putting students in groups and imploring them to work nicely together is more likely to result in chaos, frustration, and misbehavior than in learning. Five crucial elements are needed to transform the individualistic, competitive classroom into a collaborative, engaging learning environment:

1. Culture
2. Accountability
3. Process
4. Goals
5. Skillfulness

Culture

The classroom culture establishes the context for collaborative learning—or not. Students, regardless of their age or ability, are keenly aware of the context within which teaching and learning happen from one classroom to the next. Where there is no explicit message about what is important or expected, implicit messages will prevail. If there are explicit messages (classroom rules, talk about cooperation, a sign on the wall lauding teamwork), but the behaviors of the teachers, staff, and students don't match, the behaviors will prevail every time. Thus, it is the congruency of the messages, both implied and expressed, that will set the tone and culture of the classroom environment.

Creating a classroom culture of engagement and cooperation begins with the teacher's leadership style and expectations. A classic study conducted by Kurt Lewin in the early 1900s contrasted leaders with autocratic and democratic styles and looked at the impact they had on groups of children in a boys' club. The autocratic leaders "dominated meetings, set goals, issued instructions, interrupted, made all decisions, and criticized the work. Their followers argued more, showed more hostility, fought, damaged play materials, lost initiative, and showed no concern for group goals or others' interests" (as cited in Weisbord, 1991, p. 83). The democratic leaders "encouraged groups to set goals, make decisions, and mutually critique one another's work. These groups stuck to the task and developed more group spirit and cooperation" (as cited in Weisbord, 1991, p. 83). When the leaders left the room, the boys in the autocratic group picked on weaker members, goofed off, and destroyed their work. In the democratic group, the boys hardly noticed the leaders' absence—they kept on working. Moreover, democratic leaders got results, not just because of their style, but because they required a goal focus and an action orientation. There is a systemic finding in these studies that suggests that the interaction of democratic leadership within a group that is focused on a common task or goal could alter the attitudes and actions of all those in a particular social system (for example, a school) more quickly than individuals acting in isolation (as cited in Weisbord, 1991).

Teachers can promote more democratic cultures in their classrooms with the identification of a set of clear norms or agreements, developed collaboratively with and by the students. Start by having students draw a picture of what teamwork looks like. What elements of a team make it successful? If you are working with younger students who may not have had an opportunity to play on an organized team, help them think about a time when they played well with a sibling, friend, or grandparent. If they can connect their experiences with ideas about how a collaborative classroom would look, they'll be able to identify what their role needs to be to make it a reality. For older students, the opportunity to define what collaboration looks like, sounds like, and feels like (Gibbs, 1995) can result in a clear set of expectations and agreed-upon commitments for working together.

To learn more about building collaborative classroom cultures, refer to the following resources:

- *The Caring Classroom* by Laurie S. Frank (2001)

- *Tribes: A New Way of Learning and Being Together* by Jeanne Gibbs (1995)

- *Capturing Kids' Hearts* by the Flippen Group (2010)

Accountability

In addition to identifying norms, students should talk about how they will hold themselves and each other accountable to those norms, as well as what the teacher's role will be in supporting and reinforcing the norms. They agree on some simple signals such as holding up a symbol for letting the teacher or a classmate know when a norm is being violated. Of course, these signals need to be subtle and done in a spirit of support as opposed to finger pointing or blame. To be clear, this is not your garden-variety behavior management program. This practice is about building shared responsibility for learning in a collaborative, highly focused, and caring classroom community.

Accountability itself can become a collaborative endeavor. An example of a classroom practice that instills shared responsibility is the assignment and use of accountability partners. In the true spirit of partnership, students buddy up to support each other's learning, to check in on each other's progress, and to collaborate on various tasks or projects. When incorporated into the regular, ongoing procedures for learning management, the use of accountability partners becomes a predictable and valued aspect of student learning communities.

Accountability should be a cause for celebration, especially when it is attached to a common, collaboratively developed goal. As students monitor their progress as individuals and as a community of learners, each step closer to the goal is a sign of growth—and a reason to celebrate. Students quickly learn that their actions link directly to results, which lead directly to feelings of self-efficacy. In the process, they also learn the value of true collaboration as a necessary skill for the 21st century learner.

Process

Collaboration that occurs in the absence of a well-defined, commonly understood process is more likely to produce frustration than results. Consider the following scenario:

> After completing his lecture on photosynthesis, Mr. Martin groups his students into project teams to complete an assigned task associated with the lesson. Students are randomly assigned to teams of

six. Each team's task reflects one aspect of the lesson; the teams are privy only to their particular task. The assignments are due at the end of the week. Time is devoted each day for teamwork.

Team A gets right to work on the task at hand. Responsibilities are divvied up by a self-appointed leader who, like the teacher, provides a deadline for the completion of each part. Individual team members go off to do their respective assignments and return on Friday (one hopes) with all of the pieces completed.

Team B doesn't know where to begin. They have no self-appointed leader, only six individuals with six different ideas of what the task entails. No one wants to be the first to volunteer for fear that he or she will be left holding the proverbial bag with no help in sight.

Team C begins by assigning roles for its first team meeting and then reviews the team project process that each has learned in another class. Step one is to be clear about what the task is, how it aligns with learning standards for the class, and the outcomes that are expected in this team's part of the assignment. Step two is an assessment of each team member's interest, knowledge, and skills associated with each aspect of the task; that way, roles and responsibilities can be determined by the group members. In step three, they create a plan with a goal, a time line, measurable benchmarks for progress, action steps, and checkpoints to monitor and track the team's progress throughout the week. Steps four and five are to implement, assess, and adjust according to the plan.

Which of these teams is most likely to feel ownership for the project? Which team is most likely to be successful in achieving the outcomes within the stated time frame? Which team is learning in community? The answer to all of these questions is obvious. The role of the *process* in bringing clarity, ownership, and ultimately a successful outcome is not so obvious—unless you're on Team A or B.

Goals

A common goal that is created collaboratively by those who will be responsible for achieving it brings direction, energy, and accountability to learning. This principle is widely known and accepted as a part of the adult PLC movement. Why would it be such a foreign notion as a classroom practice? Just as process gives clarity and ownership to the team, the goal brings focus and direction to the process. The two work hand in hand.

Goal-oriented learning gives meaning to collaboration. It's not just about a team getting an assignment done. It's about reaching for a desired result while engaging in a journey that has real merit. The journey is more meaningful, more satisfying, and more likely to end in success when the team works together to achieve the goal. Furthermore, when the goal meets the criteria of SMART and the team engages in a known and well-defined process to pursue it, the end result is not just better outcomes but more powerful learning along the way.

If we extend the use of goals beyond a given task and into classroom practice, focused, measurable, and meaningful learning begins to come together. What if the class as a whole created a goal around a particular learning standard and identified three key concepts or skills associated with that standard? Then, what if student teams were created to develop a lesson for the rest of the class on the specific indicator that they were assigned? Each team would design its own way of measuring class learning on its particular indicator and would identify a learning target for that lesson. Collectively, the three teams would know whether their ultimate goal had been met—was the class successful in meeting this learning standard? Can you see the SMART goal tree in action?

Skillfulness

Certainly the skills that are needed to do the work described previously are not innate. They are learned and honed over time and with use. Why not involve students in learning these skills within the context of real and important work as opposed to just teaching students *about* them? The best way to learn any new skill is to try it on. However, we would not expect a new driver to learn by doing; we need to teach students the skills and tools of collaboration before asking them to perform.

For very young children, the teaching and learning process associated with collaboration is more teacher-directed, but we shouldn't sell the little ones short. At a very young age, most students will engage in developmentally appropriate *collaboration*, a phenomenon that psychologists refer to as parallel play. The youngsters are in the same room, playing nicely side by side, but may not be engaged in the same activity. The next step up from parallel play is structured play. In this phase, the children play the same game but are highly dependent on the structure (rules) of the game to keep them out of conflict. Even then, referees and coaches are often necessary. At this time, the teacher might be both a teacher and a facilitator. There eventually comes a time in the evolution of play when the children realize that someone else made up the rules. In fact, if they all agree, the rules can be rewritten. Better yet, if everyone agrees, a whole new game might be created. For students who are upper elementary and beyond, the act of creating the rules of the game and defining the game itself are imperative to their engagement and leadership in the collaborative process.

At every developmental level, there are skills that students can learn and practice that will serve them in school and beyond, not just in the workplace, but as members of their communities, their families, and other important relationships. The ability to work skillfully with others to solve problems, resolve conflicts, make decisions, and create new and innovative solutions will give our young people the best chance at success no matter what their pursuit in life happens to be.

Motivation

Abraham Maslow's (1968) popular hierarchy of needs captures the basic elements of what educators have come to refer to as *the whole child*. Briefly, the levels are: nutrition, safety, social belonging, respect, and self-actualization. Each level of the hierarchy must be met before the next level is attainable. Our ultimate goal as educators is to help every child reach and sustain fulfillment at the highest level. Self-actualization means that the individual is able to achieve the full realization of his or her potential. Is that not our mission? If our mission is to create self-directed, inspired, and joyful learners who have the skills, knowledge, and desire to pursue the futures of their choice, then our classrooms must reflect that mission.

The SMART goals process coincides with what Csikszentmihalyi (1990) identified as the key factors needed to sustain student motivation at Maslow's highest level of need:

- The freedom to set clear goals that are highly meaningful to the individual,
- Having the resources to carry out the goals and becoming immersed in the act of trying to accomplish them,
- Paying attention to what is happening and making changes when necessary, and
- Enjoying immediate short-term successes while keeping an eye on the ultimate goal. (as cited in Marzano, 2003, p. 148)

To fully embed these motivational factors into everyday classroom life will require structural, procedural, and psychological changes at the school, teacher, and student levels. School leaders (principals and teacher leaders) will be responsible for orchestrating complex change aimed at building schoolwide capacity for goal-oriented classrooms. Individual classroom teachers will be responsible for leading the complex change needed to implement goal-oriented instruction. Students will be responsible for engaging in goal-oriented learning via the student SMART goals process.

It is the leader's role to ensure that the following conditions exist:

- School schedules allow time for student reflection, goal setting, and collaboration around relevant topics of interest.

- School cultures celebrate goal achievement.

- Schoolwide standards and practices provide consistent support for students at all levels of need.

- School and classroom strategies help students envision and articulate a larger purpose for their lives.

- Curriculum, instruction, and assessment practices fully engage students in the learning process.

- Instructional designs help students make personal connections to what they are learning, both experientially and relative to a larger purpose or goal in life.

- Lessons are highly engaging and self-directed.

- Goal-setting practices are aligned with self-actualization for every child.

When students know and are focused on what they need to learn, driven by what they know and are able to do, the results are almost magical, as we have learned in talking with individual students. A seventh-grade student named Sylvia told us that she used to hate school and was always in trouble. As a result of writing her own SMART goals, she knew exactly where to focus her learning. The outcome was that her grades and mastery of standards improved dramatically, giving her the confidence to aspire to be a lawyer. Haley, an eleventh grader, talked knowingly about her area of weakness in critical thinking. She described how she analyzed the way she answered questions for the necessary qualities to demonstrate that she is mastering what she's learning across subjects. Mackenzie, a fourth grader, described the process in her classroom: "Our teacher . . . gives us a paper and has us write down what we had troubles in and what we had a strong point in. If we all had the same weak point, we'd go over that a lot. If it's a strong point, we

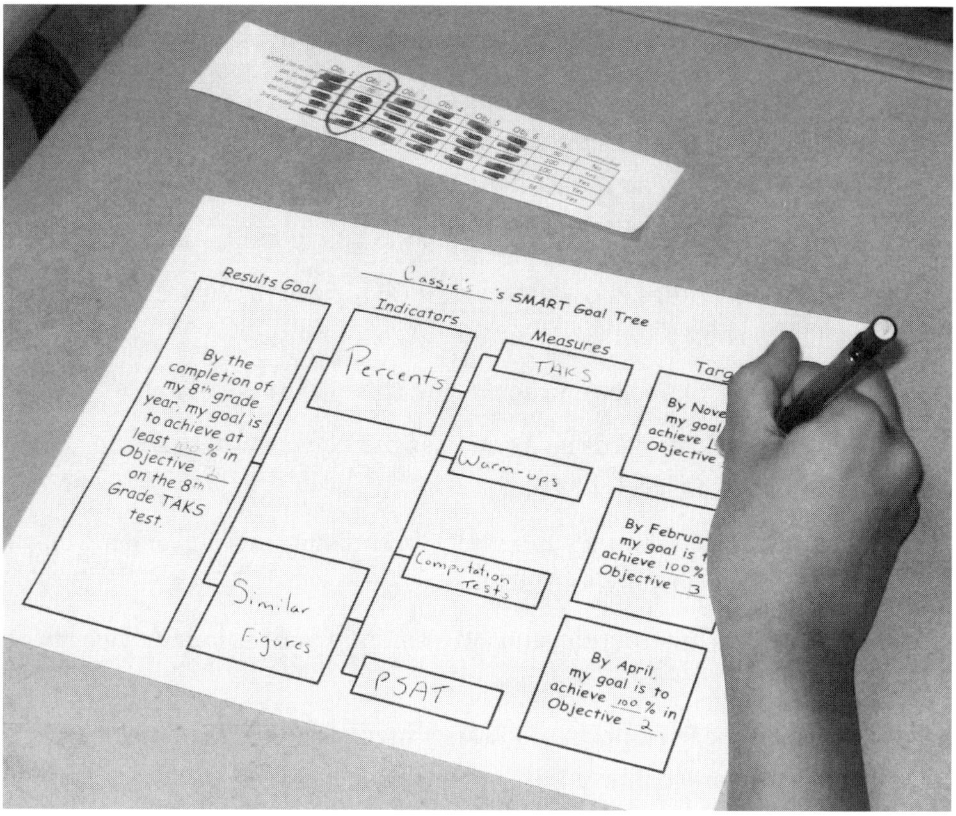

Figure 3.1: A student using a conversion chart to complete a goal tree.

wouldn't go over it so much, just review it." These students all live in a community characterized by generational poverty. Each is empowered to own her learning, and as a result, attitudes and aspirations have shifted; paths now lead to college and careers.

One of our favorite classroom stories came from a prekindergarten teacher in the same district. As the school year was coming to an end, she told her students that they had achieved their classroom SMART goal in reading. Upon hearing this, they insisted that there was time left to set and meet one more goal.

CHAPTER 4

Professional Learning by Design

If you can't describe what you are doing as a process, you don't know what you're doing.

—W. EDWARDS DEMING

Learning Forward published its "Definition of Professional Development" in 2009: "The term 'professional development' means a comprehensive, sustained, and intensive approach to improving teachers' and principals' effectiveness in raising student achievement" (Learning Forward, 2010). If we consider PLC work through the lens of the definition of *professional development*, the connection is clear. Professional development is learning through reflection on collaborative practice.

In the busy world of schools, it is easy to lose sight of the fact that the daily practice of teaching and learning holds the most potential for professional learning. The promise of such collaborative work toward the shared responsibility of student learning cannot be overstated. Oversimplification of the complexity of teachers' work leads to the misconception that learning from their practice is something teachers do in addition to their real work or that they need others to tell them what to learn and when. School-based professional learning needs to be systematically designed into collaborative structures and processes while being articulated specifically over time until "professional development that fosters collective responsibility for improved student performance" is the new norm (Learning

Forward, 2010). In this context, plans for professional learning should be:

- Coherent

- Driven by data

- Focused

- Connected to the real work of schools

These pillars of design are the foundation of effective professional learning.

Creating Supportive Structures and Schedules

It is too often the case that collaborative work that has impact is lost either because there isn't adequate time given or because time is given without common expectations that provide focus. "We're doing PLCs" or "we're using data" or "we meet as teams" may only tell part of the story. Impactful PLCs can only occur when adequate time is allocated within a school's schedule and appropriately structured for collaborative work:

> To improve student learning, schools will need structures and schedules that provide time for complex teaching and long-term relationships, conditions that give serious, ongoing assistance to learners. . . . It is unrealistic to expect that teachers will learn how to incorporate complicated practices into their repertoires on the basis of a few highly general workshops conducted after school in the school auditorium by someone who doesn't know their field, their students, or their classroom contexts, and whom they are unlikely to ever see again. (Darling-Hammond, 2008, p. 6)

Learning Forward advocates for the allocation of 25 percent of an educator's work time and about 10 percent of a district's budget for professional learning (Killion & Roy, 2009). The allocation of time for professional learning encompasses individual planning and preparation, grade-level and content team learning, school improvement meetings, and schoolwide learning. The cumulative impact of time spent on these needs should be whole-school learning and improvement.

It doesn't make sense to continue to base school calendars and schedules on the misconception that unless students are in the building, teachers are not working. Compared with teachers in other nations, American teachers spend much more time actually teaching students and significantly less time planning, learning, and developing high-quality curriculum and instruction together. U.S. teachers spend approximately 80 percent of their total working time engaged in classroom instruction versus approximately 60 percent for teachers in other nations (Darling-Hammond, Wei, Andree, Richardson, & Orphanos, 2009).

Data from the first Teaching and Learning International Survey (TALIS) indicate that American teachers—compared with teachers in high-achieving Organisation for Economic Co-operation and Development (OECD) nations—have much less time in their regular work schedules for cooperative work with colleagues. These findings suggest that while an increasing number of American teachers have opportunities for collaborative work in schools, the current structures (for example, work schedules) rarely allow for deep engagement in joint efforts to improve instruction and learning (Wei, Darling-Hammond, & Adamson, 2010).

Studies during the last decade have suggested that the length and focus both matter if professional development is going to have an impact on teaching quality and student achievement. Professional development that is sustained over time and that includes a substantial number of contact hours on a single professional development focus (averaging forty-nine hours in one multistudy review and close to one hundred in another) results in increases in student learning (Yoon, Duncan, Lee, Scarloss, & Shapley, 2007).

The average number of hours of professional development reported in the United States is only about forty-four a year. Meanwhile, teachers in many high-achieving nations are provided one hundred hours of professional development each year on top of fifteen to twenty-five hours per week for collaborative planning and learning, amounting to almost five times what U.S. teachers experience (Wei et al., 2010).

While the allocation of time is critical, the use of time is as important. In a 2009 status report, the authors (Darling-Hammond et al., 2009) recommended that professional development should:

- Be intensive, ongoing, and connected to practice
- Focus on student learning and address the teaching of specific curriculum content
- Align with school improvement priorities and goals
- Include strong working relationships among teachers

A 2009 study provides empirical evidence of the effectiveness of PLCs for increasing student achievement. The authors of this quasi-experimental longitudinal study in nine Title I schools found that using grade-level teaming with direct training of principals and teacher leaders, distributed leadership, and the use of explicit protocols increased student performance (Saunders, Goldenburg, & Gallimore, 2009). School and district leaders and policymakers should consider these characteristics when planning professional development.

A SMART Process for Professional Learning

Embedding professional learning through collaborative planning in a cycle of continuous improvement requires that we think differently, not only about time, but also about organizational structures and processes that provide feedback to inform us whether to keep going or to redirect our efforts. It is insufficient to simply allocate time and provide a schedule for meetings. Thoughtful questioning is needed on the best ways to organize:

- Who should be meeting?
- Is there a defined purpose for the meeting over time?
- How will the effectiveness of the meeting be measured?
- How are team meetings connected across the school?
- Can the faculty check themselves against what they're trying to achieve?
- Is there greater shared leadership in each team and across the school?
- How are all of these meetings serving the aim of school improvement?

While there are many processes for doing the work of school improvement, we recommend a series of meetings organized and directed by the data logic chain shown in figure 4.1.

At each step, there is a logical progression that leads to informing teachers' practice. Following this progression leads to a system of continuous improvement, which necessitates systematic processes that are dynamic in nature and sufficiently redundant so that people learn and become comfortable

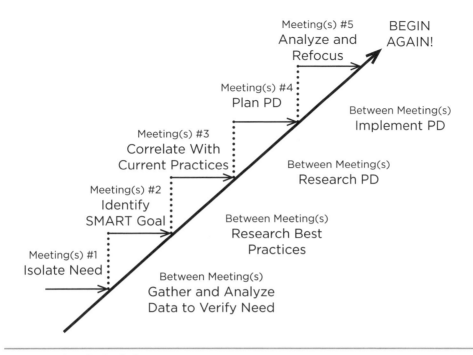

Figure 4.1: Data logic chain.

with their iterative use. Multiple meetings may be required at each step in the chain. There may be times when the progression of steps in the data logic chain can't be followed exactly, even requiring the return to a previous step to be able to move the entire effort forward. The work in between meetings (data) informs the efforts during the meetings (logic).

Isolate Need

There is nothing that drives teachers crazier than giving them lots of data while devaluing what they already know about their students. That is why we recommend that the process begin with a faculty meeting in which teachers are led through a set of activities to identify their perceptions and observations about the most significant needs of the learners in their classrooms. These perceptions are important for a number of reasons. First, we all know that perceptions are an individual's reality until they are otherwise changed by new data or a new reality. Second, fairly early in the school year, most experienced teachers know their students' strengths and where their students are struggling academically. By asking teachers to share what they already know about student performance, we honor their professionalism. Finally, when we begin with perceptual data, there is a natural tendency to want to take the next step, which is gathering the appropriate quantitative data to either verify or question what was identified qualitatively. This also allows the pursuit into the data to be much more focused as opposed to diving into reams of charts in the hope of finding something of value.

This meeting is set within the context of the work of school improvement. Its purpose is to agree upon and define the real issue. By incorporating the use of collaborative tools (for example, data trust rules and group norms), effective meeting strategies (for example, timed agendas, shared roles, and defined outcomes), and good group process techniques that fully engage all participants (for example, Affinity Diagrams, brainstorming, and multivoting), teachers will begin to feel ownership and responsibility for the process. (See Conzemius & O'Neill, 2002, for more information about these tools and methods.)

In preparation for the next step, data are gathered and analyzed to confirm or dispel the group's identified perceptions. While the group decides which potential data sources to use (for example, summative or formative assessments and attendance records), assignments are made regarding who is going to gather the data and by when. For efficiency, this is a between-meeting task.

Identify SMART Goal

After the gathered data is used to uncover the GAN, a SMART goal can be written that is strategic and specific, measurable, attainable, results based, and time bound. The act of creating a SMART goal requires a huge shift into strategic specificity; however, the act itself is not sufficient. Continuing through the process to associate indicators, measures, and targets is essential work. Using this structure and process, the team is able to create something that is actionable.

At this point, it is time to discover the best practices that address and support the SMART goal. It is important to note that the term *best practices* can be both ambiguous and multidimensional. *Best practice* should be synonymous with *effective practice*. A practice should be examined for effectiveness in the context of its practitioners, learners, and school as well as the applicable standards, assessments, and pedagogy. The group must decide upon the criteria for best practices as well as the dimension(s) on which to focus—what they're teaching (curriculum), how they're teaching it (instructional strategy), and how they are testing it (assessment). In preparation for this between-meeting work, the group members may brainstorm what they think is a best practice or agree to contact external expertise through a content specialist or use other means of research. Once assignments are made regarding what will happen, by when, and by whom, they can move on to the next step.

Correlate With Current Practices

During this meeting, the team members discuss the details of what they've discovered to be best practice. Labeling is not sufficient. Understanding the nuances among program lingo, written curricula, and standards requires team members to use a process that leads to clarity, uncovers assumptions, and results in agreement that defines what they're talking about. For example, just saying we need to use higher-order thinking is not specific enough. Teachers must define and come to an agreement about what it means in the context of the content discipline they're teaching, how they might design a lesson, and, most importantly, what student responses they are expecting. Do they know strategies to create student-to-student discussion that engages the learners with the content? Do they scaffold the content through the context of the students' discussion rather than just deliver the content? Do they know the difference between general and content discipline–specific higher-order thinking? Through teachers' collective articulation and agreement, they are able to make meaning of their current teaching practice. Once there, the process leads to data gathering as the best means for all to learn what they propose to use.

Having determined the best practice and correlated it to what they are actually doing, it is time to gather data on the best way to learn how to improve their practice by researching options for professional development. The old definition of professional development would have had members scrambling to find a class. The new definition encourages them to consider examining student work, observing each other's classrooms, videotaping, using a protocol such as critical friends, or utilizing an instructional coach. There are myriad opportunities that should be researched to discover the one that best fits what they want to learn and their desired method of learning it. Group members assigned to this task bring potential methods to the group's next meeting.

Plan Professional Development

This is professional development in the contemporary sense—professional learning that is often accomplished with and through peers, for which time and resources have been provided, employing action research and study over time as opposed to simply attending a training event. Two questions that need to be addressed in planning professional development are:

1. How is the team going to learn these strategies to ensure effective application in classrooms?

2. When and where will the team learn these strategies?

The work now begins of actually employing what the team has decided that it is going to learn. This is the best of job-embedded professional development. Teachers are learning with their peers on a daily basis, incorporating the best practices they've identified specific to the students that they're actually teaching. It takes the abstraction out of who, what, when, how, and, perhaps most important, why they are participating in professional development.

Analyze and Refocus

Measuring the effects of an instructional strategy on student learning using an agreed-upon assessment requires that the team as a whole examines the impact that the strategy had on both student and teacher learning. For example, a team can choose to administer a common assessment or gather samples of student work to share. All of the members of a team should examine the impact on both the individual teacher's application and the team's collective application against meaningful measures of student learning. This deepens the team members' understanding of what both they and their students have learned and what remains to be learned. Because the cycle of continuous improvement is happening close to the actual work of teaching and learning, gathering data to determine whether improvement actually happened can be expeditious and effective.

Cycle Back and Begin Again

The same processes that are used by a faculty to define and use their SMART school improvement goal can be used across an entire system, by PLCs, and by teachers in the classroom to get students involved in both classroom and student goal setting. While the goal itself is important, the conversation, data analyses, and collaborative thinking that go into its creation and use are equally important.

Leading for Implementation

Making any initiative successful requires a village that is willing to commit to purposefully act toward a common outcome. Collaborating stakeholders working cross-functionally and interdependently create the conditions for their work to gain momentum. Meaningful implementation occurs when the group recommits by staying the course and adjusting as needed throughout the journey.

District Leaders

Districts that produce consistently high student achievement operate within defined autonomy, which means that "the superintendent expects building principals and all other administrators in the district to lead *within the boundaries defined by the district goals*" (Marzano & Waters, 2009, p. 8). District goals represent a broader vision of what is most desired and, as such, provide goal-setting parameters and direction for the rest of the system. District goals tend to be longer term (for example, five years out) than building or grade-level goals and generally are measured using annual, summative measures. Additionally, district goals speak to the organization as a whole, which allows campus-, grade-, and department-level goals to address site-based needs in specific areas of performance. SMART goals at the district level strategically focus the district's work on its greatest area of need at the macro level. This has the potential to ameliorate the common practice of working on too much at once.

Central office leaders create defined autonomy by assuring that the system of goal-driven improvement is both vertically and horizontally aligned. Without this kind of coherence and clarity from the top, schools are left to their own interpretation of what matters most, which often leads to the identification of goals that are either unconnected or potentially at cross purposes with other organizational goals. The fallout of an incoherent system has predictable negative side effects such as frustration and confusion and, in more severe cases, turnover of staff.

As a district becomes coherent and defines autonomy, the role of central office staff shifts from being deciders and providers to

> helping facilitate professional development decisions at individual schools and coordinate efforts between and among schools to maximize resources and effort without diluting individual schools' needs

and efforts. Central Office staff members have seven major tasks in a coherent system that views the school as the primary center of learning. They are:

- Build the capacity of school staff to make sound decisions;
- Provide research and models of best practices;
- Allocate resources to schools to support school learning plans;
- Coordinate efforts between and among schools' collaborative professional learning teams;
- Coordinate the formation of cross-school collaborative professional learning teams;
- Support collaborative professional learning teams;
- Monitor implementation throughout the district. (Killion & Roy, 2009, p. 68)

The Steering Committee

Once a district has chosen a strategic improvement focus, the formation of a steering committee to oversee implementation is most productive. Members should include school-based leaders as well as their central office supporters. Ideally, teacher representation offers insight into how the improvement is being perceived at the classroom level. We believe a steering committee is necessary in order to examine openly and honestly what's working and, as importantly, what's not and why in the context of the district.

The role of the steering committee is to gauge implementation of the SMART goals process using the structures and processes described. The steering committee structure allows the members to view the connections from school to school and across levels. When we consider that a child experiences schooling as prekindergarten through grade 12, but the adults are organized by levels or content, it's no wonder that schooling often feels fragmented. Examining practices among and across schools allows a district to monitor and support implementation. It is enlightening to all when, given the opportunity as a steering committee, principals and teachers intentionally step back and look at the implementation of their initiatives as a district.

The steering committee clearly showcases where implementation is going well so that practices can be illuminated and identifies rising issues so that they can be remediated before they become a roadblock to improvement. If there are roadblocks, they can be overcome. The steering committee's attention to school improvement in this manner gives a superintendent or board the confidence to stay the course and resist the temptation to jump to other initiatives. The result can be renewed energy toward the chosen path, increased student performance, and teacher and principal retention.

The Principal

Leading a 21st century school can be extraordinarily rewarding. On the other hand, being a principal can also be one of the hardest jobs on earth. Not only is there no real off time, but the job brings never-ending unexpected challenges.

Principals need to be savvy enough to protect their staff from outside distractions, while co-creating structures, schedules, and commitments in a way that blends an array of personalities and expertise. It's amazing that people still choose the role and not so amazing that there is considerable turnover in the position. According to the Institute of Education Sciences, 12 percent of principals left the principalship in 2009, and 6 percent moved to another school (Battle & Gruber, 2010).

The impact of the turnover of principals on structures and processes that support professional development and school improvement is of concern here. A school improvement teacher leader in a client school related the impact of seven new principals over a six-year period. From her perspective, the constant change in the principal's office became an overwhelming dynamic that obscured the improvement process. When she looked past the frustrations of the constant change, she was able to see that the process was moving ahead, albeit much more slowly than she would otherwise have expected. Turnover in the principal's office can work against the development of shared leadership and commitment to a common purpose.

Leadership begins with understanding that every gathering is an opportunity to deepen accountability and commitment through engagement (Block, 2008). Principals who understand this create opportunities for meaningful interactions within structures and processes. They also seek opportunities that spontaneously occur during their day to encourage learning, reflection, and trust. Improvement is a process, not a destination.

School Teams

A cornerstone of effective schools is shared leadership. According to James Spillane (2005), leadership is distributed over an interactive web of people and situations that frames leadership practice in a particular way: "Distributive leadership is first and foremost about leadership practice rather than leaders or their roles, functions, routines, and structures. . . . Leadership *practice* is viewed as a product of the interactions of school leaders, followers, and their situation." From this perspective, the work of grade-level or content teams, plus school leadership teams when strategically focused, can and should lead to improved and improving student performance and ownership of the work of the school. In this way, a school assumes its right and responsibility to ensure that all students are successful.

A school-based leadership team, what we refer to as a SMART leadership team, is tasked with overseeing the implementation of SMART goals in the context of school improvement at the school. The team could be formed for this purpose or could be an existing improvement team. As with the district steering committee, the team is most effective when it meets regularly and focuses the agenda on assessing implementation. When a team is given the opportunity to share leadership by developing trust, monitoring progress, and finding common solutions, the result is shared responsibility, commitment, and accountability for success.

Sometimes teacher teams are organized and have time to meet but lack the purpose and process to make their work impactful. Co-constructing a common understanding of shared purpose and committing to processes that allow for depth of work and cross-team communication merits the time. That is how an effective school team can sustain itself and improve student learning.

Snapshot of a District

We partner with districts to intentionally build their capacity for sustainability. An example of a client district that continues to successfully implement the SMART goals process on their own tells the story of how this is done. Commitment to the SMART goals process has changed the way the district works in the central office and across the schools, with impact seen from the school board to the prekindergarten students. Use of the process continues to change the generational poverty in the community by improving the schools. Students who previously were apathetic about their education are now becoming the first generation to go to college. The change wasn't due to magic. It was the product of hard work. It took a board's commitment and a superintendent's vision to make hard decisions and stay the course. It took district leadership that wanted to learn the SMART goals methodology and build capacity so that they could eventually sustain and lead the work. It took stamina on the part of principals to lead both themselves and their faculties through new learning. It took dedicated teachers who became increasingly enthusiastic and committed when they saw their students succeeding.

District leadership committed to align everything to the successful implementation of the SMART goals process. This meant examining what they already had in place, discarding what no longer fit, and introducing new district initiatives that would integrate successfully. They established nonnegotiable parameters while supporting learning. They incorporated new state mandates and stayed on top of data. They made sure that the curriculum was aligned and articulated, that assessments were in place to provide feedback, and that professional development was provided. They helped change school schedules, acted as substitutes in classes, and mentored students. They created time for teachers to meet. They created a system to orient new staff members. They learned how to coach in the SMART goals process. They supported new learning by holding up a vision for success, required everyone to use this process, and highlighted successes, both large and small.

Over time, people throughout the district took ownership for using the SMART goals process in ways that worked. The junior high school principal created time for teachers to meet during the school day. Consistent application of the SMART goals process led the teachers to analyze their students' work and share instructional strategies at a new level. Textbooks became resources instead of the key driver of the written curriculum. When this principal moved to the high school, he created a schedule that allowed for core academic teachers to meet during the day. The high school started to see the same results. Teachers across the system began viewing their team time as professional learning.

During their team time, teachers saw their data in new ways. The ambiguous statement "use data to inform your instruction" was unpacked through a process that created understanding about what the data were actually saying. When teachers become proficient in the continuous improvement cycle and use it to inform what they need to learn and be able to do well, they focus their professional learning. A district teacher reported to the school board, "I now know what aspect of the curriculum I teach well and what I need help with. My repertoire of instructional strategies has expanded as I work with my team. We own all of the students at our grade level now. If one student isn't 'getting it' from me, I'll ask if he or she can sit in on the lesson taught by another teacher."

Structures for communicating with parents also became more meaningful. A board member noted that she and her son now talk about his schoolwork in relation to his SMART goal. Parents are asked to sign forms, acknowledging that they know what their child's SMART goal is and creating opportunities for parent-student conversations to go beyond the frequently asked question, "Is your homework done?" This parent-informed and involved approach also resulted in a change of tenor at the district's parent-teacher conferences.

Helping a district succeed requires meaningful ways of providing feedback. Adding a system that measures impact and implementation provides consistent feedback and a clearer course of action.

CHAPTER 5

Impact and Implementation

If gold represents the vision, then platinum represents the implementation.

—Douglas B. Reeves

While helping schools and districts master the SMART goals process, we discovered that we needed to provide assistance way beyond training and coaching. Districts need support to help them situate SMART-goal writing and its use within the larger context of their work. Goals themselves don't drive improvement; they must be aligned to the school improvement process, curriculum, instruction, assessment practices, mandates, and professional development. In order for goals to gain enough traction to have an impact, there must be a system that keeps us continuously focused on them. Indeed, unless we're seeing short-term gains and increasing clarity regarding how we can work smarter, we soon become discouraged and move off course. It takes discipline at the beginning of new learning to stick to the methodology to gain momentum. This not only produces results but also increases our energy and excitement to see just how successful we can be.

The alignment of focus throughout a system, whether it is school to teachers to students or—even more exciting—district to schools to teachers to students, can change the landscape of a community. Choosing a focus and staying with it long enough to have it become systemic requires courage and conviction (Fullan, 2010). True systemic work is a level III fix—redesigning the system instead of just putting out fires (level I fixes)—and requires a leader who has the positional authority, influence, and perseverance to stay the course. Our goal is to build the capacity of schools and school systems so that they learn how to implement a systemic process that provides focus and impacts learning at every level, including the level of individual students.

Why Measure?

What if we *don't* achieve the goal? There are many reasons why an intervention or an initiative does not produce the hoped-for results. If we're setting goals that are worth pursuing, we may not always reach them on the first try. The important thing is that we learn from each attempt that is made and then make adjustments as we go. To do so requires that we have a system in place for knowing whether we're making progress toward the goal along the way.

We also need to create the kind of environment in which it's OK to ask tough questions, such as:

- Was it the right intervention for the need?
- Did we identify the right problem in the first place?
- Did we know what was causing the problem?
- Did we actually implement the intervention or solution as planned?
- Did we do so with fidelity?
- Were there systemic issues that prevented the intervention or strategy from being implemented well?

These are fundamental questions that make up a robust analysis of any improvement strategy.

What if we *do* achieve the goal? There are equally as many reasons why an intervention or initiative does produce the hoped-for results. In this case, we want to know what to replicate, take to scale, or standardize. The trick lies in gathering the right evidence or data and then ferreting out potential conclusions based on what we know works and why.

Because we are dealing with very complex systems, it is almost impossible to say for certain that any one initiative has caused an improvement or has directly led to a particular result. While purely empirical studies are possible in education, they cannot tell the whole story because, by their very nature, they are controlled and narrowly focused. So, the best we can do is be systematic about what gets measured and how it gets measured and put multiple forms of evidence into the mix in order to see the system that is producing the results.

The capricious nature of public education makes it challenging for individuals within a district to have an impact. Employing even the best methods to organize, train, and coach, those charged with implementing the selected initiative can easily veer off course unless there is a system to keep them focused by measuring implementation and impact along the way. The critical juncture is what gets done with the information that is fed back, how it is fed back, and to whom. Michael Fullan's (2010) words in *Motion Leadership* are timely and to the point: "Now it is time to see the concise meaning of getting peers to interact on a focused basis" (p. 35). Having common instruments (for example, an evidenced-based rubric or TurboMeeting agenda) that help to focus these conversations without making them overly controlled can accelerate the change process and keep implementation on track. The consistent examination of where we are against where we want to go allows us to continuously mediate our actions. How simple it would be if it were a straight path from here to there.

School-based continuous improvement through PLCs has become the norm. It's almost hard to remember BPLC (before PLCs). However, having impactful PLCs is another matter. Richard DuFour and Robert Eaker have done an admirable job helping schools aspire to be professional learning communities, beginning with *Professional Learning Communities at Work*™ in 1998. Shirley Hord (1997) contributed to the research base and identified the attributes of a PLC, stating that the purpose of PLCs is the learning of adults and professionals as it impacts student learning. However, school districts have spun their wheels in the name of PLCs, lacking both strategic focus and clarity of process. Strategic focus must align the work of PLCs with the aim of the system as defined by a district's instructional priorities. As important, there must be a common and clear process for improvement used by the members of PLCs. Finally, the impact of and across PLCs must be measured if the district is to know if it is accomplishing the learning goals.

Models of Evaluation

Measuring change resulting from something new (innovation, improvement, initiative) has been a viable, though not always widely used, methodology in education for many years. A respected, well-researched model for doing so is the Concerns Based Adoption Model (CBAM). The three dimensions of the CBAM are (1) stages of concern, (2) levels of use, and (3) innovation configurations. Table 5.1 summarizes the components of this model for measuring change, its implementation, and its suggested use.

Table 5.1: CBAM Instruments, Description, and Use

Instrument	Description and Use
Stages of concern questionnaire	A valid, reliable instrument that measures the seven stages of concerns practitioners experience during change efforts. Measures the intensity of the concerns using three clusters: self, task, impact.
Levels of use	Measures behavioral changes through eight stages of use (nonuse, orientation, preparation, mechanical use, routine, refinement, integration, renewal)
Innovation configurations	Rubric-like tool that identifies and describes various forms of an innovation (or improvement). Used for introducing a change as well as monitoring its implementation.

Source: Adapted from Hall & Hord, 2011.

Thomas Guskey's (2000) work bridged the gap between educational research and practice, giving us a way to evaluate professional development. In his five critical levels of professional development evaluation, he applies Donald Kirkpatrick's (1998) four levels of evaluating training models (reaction, learning, behavior, and results) to education and builds on them by inserting organization support to create five levels. Table 5.2 reflects the combined contributions of Guskey and Kirkpatrick.

Joellen Killion (2008) continued to build this model by adding return on investment, creating the six levels of training evaluation seen in table 5.3 (page 96).

Killion also gives us a model to evaluate professional development:

1. Planning phase

   □ Assess evaluability.

   □ Formulate evaluation questions.

   □ Construct the evaluation framework.

2. Conducting phase

   □ Collect data.

   □ Organize, analyze, and display data.

   □ Interpret data.

Table 5.2: Guskey's Five Critical Levels of Professional Development Evaluation

Evaluation Level	What Is Measured or Assessed	How Will Information Be Used
Participants' reactions	Initial satisfaction with experience	To improve program design and delivery
Participants' learning	New knowledge and skills of participants	To improve program content, format, and organization
Organization support and changes	The organization's advocacy, support, accommodation, facilitation, and recognition	To document and improve organizational support To inform future changes
Participants' use of new knowledge and skills	Degree and quality of implementation	To document and improve the implementation of program content
Student learning outcomes	Student learning outcomes: Cognitive (performance and achievement) Affective (attitudes and dispositions) Psychomotor (skills and behaviors)	To focus and improve all aspects of program design, implementation, and follow-up To demonstrate the overall impact of professional development

Source: Adapted from Guskey, 2000, pp. 79–81

3. Reporting phase

    ▫ Disseminate and use findings.

    ▫ Evaluate the evaluation.

A powerful construct offered by Killion (2008) distinguishes between black-box and glass-box evaluations:

> Black-box evaluations focus on results rather than what occurs in the program or what is presumed to be causing those outcomes and why. In a black-box evaluation, the evaluator is interested only in knowing whether the outcome occurred and not in helping the program stakeholders understand how the program produced results. . . .
>
> Glass-box evaluations illuminate how a staff development program's components interact to produce results. Glass-box evaluation provides information on what occurs and how it occurs within a program. The effectiveness of a staff development program is strengthened when both its implementation and its impact are evaluated. . . . A glass-box evaluation of staff development provides the information needed for making adjustments and improvements and for increasing the probability of producing the intended results for students. (pp. 24, 25)

Table 5.3: Killion's Levels of Evaluation of Training

Levels 1–6	Sample Evaluation Questions	Value of Information	Frequency of Use	Difficulty of Assessment
1. Measuring reaction to the learning experience (Guskey, 2000; Kirkpatrick, 1998)	Were participants satisfied with the learning experience?	Least valuable	Frequent	Easy
2. Measuring learning (Guskey, 2000; Kirkpatrick, 1998)	What did the participants learn?			
3. Assessing organizational support and change (Guskey, 2000)	How has the culture of the school changed?			
4. Assessing application of learning (Guskey, 2000; Kirkpatrick, 1998)	How often are participants implementing the new practices?			
5. Assessing student learning (Guskey, 2000; Kirkpatrick, 1998)	Has student achievement increased?			
6. Calculating return on investment (Phillips, 1997)	What is the fiscal return on stakeholders' investment?	Most valuable	Infrequent	Difficult

Source: Killion, 2008, p. 39. Used with permission.

Through glass-box evaluation, we can determine whether selected interventions, based on scientific research or not, have merit (achieved the intended results), worth (are perceived as valuable), or impact.

These models for measuring use, change, implementation, and impact resulting from an initiative or intervention are constructs that helped inform our work as we began designing our SMART Measurement System.

SMART Measurement System (SMS)

The SMART Measurement System (SMS) is a glass-box evaluation that has three critical components: (1) results, (2) strategic focus, and (3) leadership capacity. It is used by a steering committee or other leadership group to measure impact over the course of implementation. While it was developed with the SMART goals process in mind, the SMS can be used to measure the impact of any improvement initiative. The SMS is comprised of different but complementary measures and tools that encourage investigation of the depth of implementation of the SMART goals process. With SMS, we can determine to what degree the SMART goals process is being used to impact student learning. Armed with this information, implementation can be deepened.

Figure 5.1 shows the various attributes and tools of SMS.

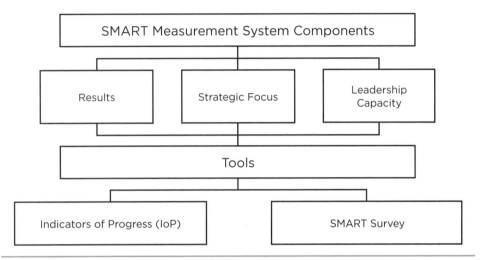

Figure 5.1: SMS components.

The SMART goal tree serves, in this context, as a graphic organizer for the various elements of SMS, as shown in figure 5.2 (page 98).

When we begin our work with a steering committee, we ask the committee to set a SMART goal using the following format:

By _____ (year), _____ % of our teachers will have adopted the SMART goals process as their professional improvement practice.

The act of creating this SMART goal brings clarity and commitment to the use of the process. The discussion that leads to this decision often uncovers assumptions, beliefs, and barriers. As an example, a district initially set its goal at 65 percent of the teachers; six months into the process, the goal was increased to 85 percent of the teachers after the district discovered the impact of the process. The superintendent of another district took a crucial leadership stance when he challenged his steering committee to think in terms of 100 percent of the district's teachers.

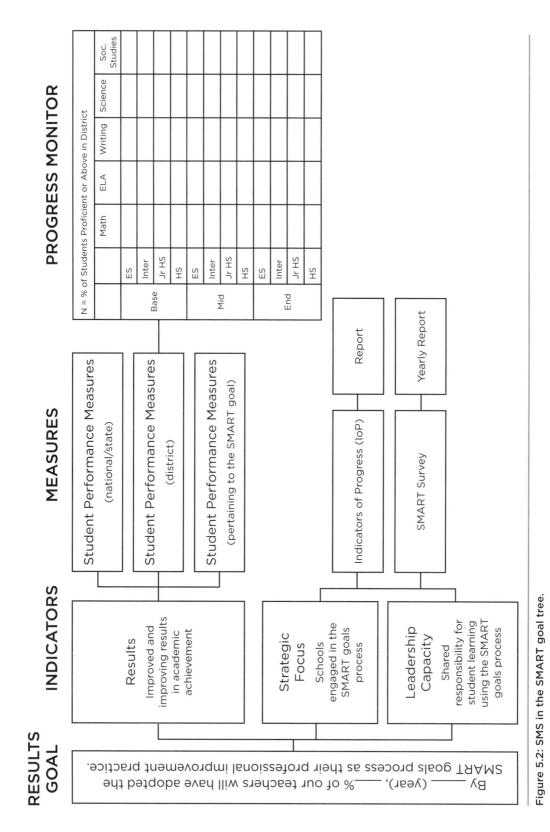

Figure 5.2: SMS in the SMART goal tree.

Results

Improved and improving results in academic achievement is where the rubber meets the road. Measuring the degree to which an initiative is being implemented can be done using instruments like rubrics and walkthroughs and by examining student work. However, the critical bottom line is whether student performance is increasing.

The student performance data used by a steering committee at the district level begins with the results of national and state high-stakes tests. Because these data are so visible, it would be delusional to think that they are not a primary focus of school districts. However, district benchmarks and other measures of K–12 student performance pertaining to a district SMART goal are also critical gauges of a school district's progress. Data from all of these measures across time, subpopulations, and grade levels should be investigated. Measuring results along the way is important input to changing practice at all levels, from the classroom to the district. How else would you know how to stay on course toward improvement?

Strategic Focus

Strategic focus is dependent on what the district has chosen as its process for change. We articulate strategic change over time along a continuum from inquiry to institutionalization, incorporating Fullan's (1991) three stages of change (initiation, implementation, and institutionalization) and expanded by Abplanalp (2007) with the addition of the inquiry stage. Abplanalp added *inquiry* because she discovered that "some staff were not even at the Initiation stage" (p. 43). Based on these works, we define the four stages of change as follows:

1. **Inquiry**—A team or person at this stage is still questioning the process. While there may be a belief that change needs to occur, there is no commitment to participate in it.

2. **Initiation**—The initiation phase is the beginning process of change. Teams understand the need and have begun active participation in the change process. New strategies are being tried in the classroom, during team meetings, or in both. A person at this level has made a commitment to moving forward.

3. **Implementation**—Teams during the implementation phase are well on their way to understanding the new process. They are

enthusiastic about the process and are coordinating efforts to make changes in their classrooms, during team meetings, or in both. Teams at this level seek ongoing technical assistance, often putting pressure on others to join and support the initiative. A person at this level sees the change as an expectation and shared responsibility in the SMART goals process.

4. **Institutionalization**—By this phase, teams have embedded the new strategies, tools, and processes in the way they work together and in their classroom practices. They understand all aspects of the process and place a high priority on their own continuous learning and improvement. The process has become "the way we do our work here."

Leadership Capacity

We have worked with districts and schools to build shared responsibility for student learning for many years. As an outcome of our work, we have identified five critical attributes that have the greatest impact on the creation of successful teams:

1. Shared accountability

2. Shared vision

3. Shared commitment to building trust

4. Shared leadership

5. Shared focus of professional learning

Note the emphasis on the word *shared*—without that critical dimension, the work is not that of a team. It is critical to help teams analyze how functional they are in doing their work in the context of improved and improving student performance and the degree to which they are building shared responsibility.

SMS Tools

Two SMS tools address strategic focus and leadership capacity, providing additional information and augmenting student learning results. The tools of the SMS are: the Indicators of Progress™ (IoP™) rubric and the SMART Survey™. The SMS is designed for progress monitoring at a system level. The IoP is an evidence-based rubric that is used on an ongoing basis for progress monitoring. School teams examine the IoP for the purpose of analyzing their own growth and providing fodder for coaching. The SMART Survey is an annually administered perceptual instrument that supplies feedback from the whole school staff and their SMART leadership team. The feedback from the survey allows each school to see how the whole school is being impacted. It is used for assessing how deeply the SMART goals process is being developed throughout a school. Over time, the SMART Survey provides a source of information that monitors and guides progress toward full implementation. Cumulatively, individual school surveys provide feedback to the district and to those who are funding the process by measuring the depth of the implementation and identifying additional resources that might be needed or changes they might need to make. Through the use of these tools, districts are able to determine the ROI in money, time, and people.

Indicators of Progress

The IoP, an evidence-based rubric, is an instrument used to help teams analyze where they are, make decisions in each of the domains where they should focus to deepen implementation, and determine what actions they will take. It is a vehicle for focused coaching and provides an anchor for the team's ongoing conversations between sessions. Evidence helps the SMART leadership team articulate where its focus connects to the other work that schools and their teams are doing. For example, if a school is low performing and has state-mandated plans and required documentation, the leadership team must connect these to the SMART goals process. Evidence within the IoP should include documentation, including work on school improvement plans and other plans mandated by the federal government and the provincial or state department of education.

A SMART leadership team collectively analyzes each dimension of the IoP—results, strategic focus, and leadership capacity—literally highlighting where they are. As they examine across the levels, rich conversation and shared understanding of the SMART goals process and its implementation occur. This leads to two critical questions: (1) what is our evidence?, and (2) what actions do we need to take for implementation to be successful? First, using the IoP helps the team agree on what will constitute evidence. This may include, but is not limited to, benchmark data analyses for results, classroom walkthroughs for strategic focus, and team meeting minutes for leadership capacity. It is important that the team decides what is meaningful as this is what builds its capacity for shared responsibility and leadership.

Second, having determined where it is, it develops a plan for action. Actions could include discussing its IoP evidence at a faculty meeting and asking a coach to observe team meetings. Team members determine what is needed to move their work to the next level. The IoP is designed to be used as a map. It's important to consult it regularly until the terrain is well known.

The sharing of IoPs across teams within a school assists the collection of evidence about the school as a whole. If math is a school's greatest area of need, it is important to measure the progress of each team. For example, are the sixth-, seventh-, and eighth-grade math teams each progressing? Are their rates similar? Are the barriers that need to be overcome for all teams or just one? Is there a need for additional support or resources? Use of the IoP for organizing evidence helps the principal, the SMART leadership team, coaches, and central office know how to best support progress.

Figure 5.3 shows an example of an IoP.

SMART Survey

The use of a survey to measure perceptions or opinions can be a valuable, low-threat method of getting feedback. Online surveys are easily constructed and administered. To increase participation rates, require participation and monitor it during the period when the survey is open. The survey should be administered periodically throughout the course of implementation to measure the degree of cultural change. It is made clear to the survey respondents that their answers are anonymous. (See *The Handbook for SMART School Teams* [Conzemius & O'Neill, 2002] for further guidance on the construction of quality surveys.)

In the SMART Survey, 144 items are organized around four factors (36 items for each factor): (1) focus, (2) reflection, (3) collaboration, and (4) leadership capacity. Following are example items from each.

1. **Focus:** Our teams (grade level/department) are studying and improving our instructional practices in our team SMART goal.

2. **Reflection:** Our school uses zones to analyze aggregated and disaggregated data over time for our school SMART goal.

3. **Collaboration:** In our school, trust and openness characterize the way we work.

4. **Leadership capacity:** Each member of our team actively contributes to the SMART goals process.

SMART Goals Process
Indicators of Progress (IoP)

Purpose: An evidence-based tool to show growth over time. This tool will provide feedback to you as a team, to the coach, and to the steering committee.

Use: SMART leadership and professional learning teams should use the IoP as a guiding document and as a way to measure their progress. We recommend that it's used a minimum of three to four times per year.

	Definition of Levels
Level 1 **Inquiry**	A team or person at this stage is still questioning the process. While there may be a belief that change needs to occur, there is no commitment to participate in it.
Level 2 **Initiation**	The initiation phase is the beginning process of change. Teams understand the need and have begun active participation in the change process. New strategies are being tried in the classroom, during team meetings, or in both. A person at this level has made a commitment to moving forward.
Level 3 **Implementation**	Teams during the implementation phase are well on their way to understanding the new process. They are enthusiastic about the process and are coordinating efforts to make changes in their classrooms, during team meetings, or in both. Teams at this level seek ongoing technical assistance, often putting pressure on others to join and support the initiative. A person at this level sees the change as an expectation and shared responsibility in the SMART goals process.
Level 4 **Institutionalization**	By this phase, teams have embedded the new strategies, tools, and processes in the way they work together and in their classroom practices. They understand all aspects of the process and place a high priority on their own continuous learning and improvement. It has become "the way we do our work here."

Sources: Levels adapted from Michael Fullan's (1991) The New Meaning of Educational Change and Sue Abplanalp's (2007) Breaking the Low-Achieving Mindset. Rubric format adapted from NSDC's Innovation Configurations for professional learning communities (Roy & Hord, 2003).

NOTES:

- The term *professional learning teams* refers to grade-level, subject-matter, interdisciplinary, or vertical teams of teachers that collaborate to improve student learning.

- The SMART acronym stands for *specific and strategic, measurable, attainable, results based, time bound.*

- The GAN acronym stands for *greatest area of need* and refers to the academic/achievement area that is most in need of improvement.

continued →

Figure 5.3: IoP.

Baseline Data: _____ Progress Check Data: _____ Results Data: _____

Indicators of Progress (IoP)

	Inquiry	Initiation	Implementation	Institutionalization	Examples of Evidence
Results: Improved and improving results in academic achievement					
Student Performance Data	Evidence indicates aggregate student performance movement toward the SMART goal.	Evidence indicates disaggregate student performance improvement by zones, reducing the gap in the GAN.	Evidence indicates disaggregate student performance improvement by zones, reducing the gap in the GAN using multiple measures.	Evidence indicates disaggregate student performance improvement by zones, reducing the gap in the GAN using multiple measures over time.	What evidence do you have in established improvement plans?
Strategic focus: Schools engaged in the SMART goals process					
	Inquiry	Initiation	Implementation	Institutionalization	Examples of Evidence
School SMART Goals Process	A goal exists that meets the SMART criteria. It may or may not have been developed by the school staff. The goal is part of a plan but is not used to monitor progress.	The school is doing the work associated with the SMART goals process (analyzing data, writing goals, researching best practices, engaging in professional development), but the work is being done as a separate instead of a coherent process that is connected to other improvement initiatives (PLC).	The school SMART goal is based on the school's GAN. Supporting goals are aligned with the school goal. School staff is analyzing school data, monitoring progress in their GAN, researching best practices, and engaging in professional development aligned to their SMART goal.	The school SMART goal is based on the school's GAN. Supporting goals are aligned with the school goal. School staff is analyzing school data, monitoring progress in their GAN, researching best practices, and engaging in professional development aligned to their SMART goal. There is a system in place for the school to continuously engage in this cycle. Students are active participants in the school SMART goals process.	What information will you collect to show use of the SMART goals process at the school level?

Team SMART Goals Process	Teachers generally base their lessons on data and incorporate new activities learned from their colleagues.	The team is doing the work associated with the SMART team process (analyzing data, writing goals, developing common assessments, creating lessons, engaging in root cause analysis), but the work is being done as separate, unconnected pieces, instead of as a coherent process that is connected to their goal.	The team SMART goals reflect student needs as determined by staff analysis of district benchmark and classroom data. Teams are monitoring progress in their GAN. Teams have created and administered a common assessment based on essential learning standards and have lessons aligned to their SMART goal. Teams have determined probable root cause(s) for learning gaps.	The team SMART goals reflect student needs as determined by analysis of commonly used assessment data. Teams are monitoring progress in their GAN. Teams have created and administered a common assessment based on essential learning standards and have lessons aligned to their SMART goal. Teams have determined probable root cause(s) for learning gaps. There is a continuous cycle of improvement that incorporates differentiation and lesson adjustments. Students are active participants in the team/classroom SMART goals process.	What information will you collect to show use of the SMART goals process at the professional learning team level?
Student SMART Goals Process	Students write a goal that may or may not be based on their data.	Students write SMART goals that are based on their data and monitor their learning targets.	Students write a SMART goal for each subject area that is based on their data and monitor their learning targets. They may or may not adjust their learning targets accordingly. Teams of students may or may not share their learning strategies with each other.	Students are looking at their individual and classroom data and developing their own SMART goals for each subject. Students are monitoring their progress and continuously adjusting their targets and learning strategies accordingly. Teams of students are sharing their learning strategies with each other. Students are active participants in all levels of the SMART goals process.	What information will you collect to show use of the SMART goals process at the student level?

continued →

Leadership capacity: Shared responsibility for student learning using the SMART goals process

	Inquiry	Initiation	Implementation	Institutionalization	Examples of Evidence
Shared Accountability	Individuals are responsible for their own students.	Teacher teams meet to discuss data on students or curricula they have in common.	Schoolwide forums exist for teachers to discuss curriculum, instruction, and assessment practices. Data on student performance are analyzed by grade-level or department teams.	Schoolwide forums exist for all members of the school faculty and staff to discuss curriculum, instruction, and assessment practices. All members of the school faculty and staff take collective action to assist students in developing, learning, and achieving at high levels.	What artifacts will you collect that indicate shared accountability?
Shared Vision	There is a school vision statement.	A small group is involved in developing and communicating a school vision statement.	The vision is developed by the full faculty and staff.	The entire school faculty and staff are engaged in the development and monitoring of a school vision. Actions, decisions, and goals are aligned in support of the school vision.	What artifacts will you collect to show evidence of shared vision?
Shared Commitment to Building Trust	Teachers smile and nod and talk to a select few in the parking lot.	Some teams have agreed upon a set of core values and norms for how they will work together. Individuals adhere to the norms. Individuals are honest with each other and have made a commitment to working through their differences in productive ways.	Some teams and individuals honestly and skillfully share their agreements and disagreements with the entire faculty in a way that builds trust.	School faculty and staff have agreed upon a set of core values and norms for how they will work together. Individuals adhere to the norms. Individuals are honest with each other and have made a commitment to working through their differences in productive ways.	What artifacts will you collect to show evidence of shared commitment to building trust?
Shared Leadership	The principal is the leader of the building and is the one responsible for leading the SMART goals process.	The SMART goals process is seen as the responsibility of the SMART leadership team.	All members of the faculty and staff are involved in the SMART goals process.	All members of the school community are involved in the SMART goals process and engage in active leadership toward the achievement of their SMART goals. Forums exist where individuals and teams can share their learning with others. Leadership is broad-based and skillful.	What artifacts will you collect to show evidence of shared leadership?

Shared Focus of Professional Learning	Training occurs for the SMART leadership team. No coherent follow-up occurs with the rest of the faculty. The SMART goals process is not connected to other district initiatives and professional development.	Following training for the SMART leadership team, the whole school is brought into the process. Coaching assists with the integration of the SMART goals process into some other professional development and district initiatives.	The SMART goals process is a key driver for continuous professional learning. Members of the SMART leadership team and whole faculty are following the process at all levels.	The SMART goals process is the key driver for continuous professional learning. Collaborative learning is a cultural value. The school and district are a dynamic system that continuously builds new meaning through examination of its shared assumptions, beliefs, and practices.	What artifacts will you collect to show evidence of what your shared focus of professional learning is and how you arrived at that decision?

Purpose	Action	Who's Responsible	By When	Result/Celebration

Results from the SMART Survey are investigated during a steering committee, leadership team, or faculty meeting to determine how the rest of the school views the use of the SMART goals process. It quickly becomes evident where there is nonuse, a gap, or resistance. The steering committee is able to strategically use survey results for comparing implementation across schools or levels, for example, middle school versus high school. SMART leadership teams at the schools use the information to guide communication, coaching, and intervention. The school PLC is able to gauge commitment and make adjustments as needed. In combination with student results and data from the IoP rubric, SMART Survey results provide actionable information.

Using the SMS With Other Initiatives

Many of our examples reflect the use of the SMART goals process. However, the SMS can be used for other school-based initiatives and can also be applied in fields other than education. If you use the SMS in one of these contexts, consider the three critical attributes as follows:

1. **Results**—Identify your bottom-line desired outcome and the correlated sources of data to track.

2. **Strategic focus**—Unpack the process for improvement by developing a rubric-like instrument that includes criteria and identifies what it looks like in action from novice to expert. What must people learn and do? What are the major shifts as people deepen their practice? What is the evidence that would constitute progress?

3. **Leadership capacity**—The critical attributes of leadership capacity are shared accountability, shared vision, shared commitment to building trust, shared leadership, and shared focus of professional learning.

Applying the SMS to Gauge Implementation and Impact

So how does the SMS work in action in a real school district? After three years of SMART goals process work with a Texas district, we met for the last time with the school board for a culminating review. It was very powerful to hear teachers describe how the SMART goals process had changed their practice. Their stories gained further impact and credibility when the superintendent and other key district and campus leaders shared evidence that tracked the path of their SMART goals implementation. The SMS evidence included improving student performance data and various artifacts guided by the IoP plus results of the SMART Survey, which are reflected in figures 5.4 and 5.5 (page 110).

Peering into the glass box, our suite of vehicles included training, followed by coaching, with guidance from a steering committee. We experienced a predictable first year of implementation, during which we observed early adopters, stragglers, those who pretended to play the game, and those who were trying their best to learn the process and make it their own. Schools were coming to grips with the steps of the process, how to use it effectively, and how to work as teams using SMART goals. Principals and their leadership teams were starting to deal with the challenges of shared leadership. All of this was occurring while state-appointed technical assistance worked to get the district off *the list*. Each school's principal and leadership team was coached both in person and virtually to help them deepen their understanding of what this process looked like in practice.

During the second year, we formalized SMS and pressed it into service with dramatic results. The work of the steering committee was focused on the use of the SMS and the information contributed by each of its components. The steering committee was able to clarify what they needed to effectively implement the process. The SMS truly became the depersonalized vehicle for building trust that took the group to collegial discourse about what was best for the system, instead of blaming individuals or schools. The result was a recommitment to and increased personal accountability for staying with the process.

By the third year, the district began creating its own structures for sustaining the process. At each steering committee meeting, we posed the question of how they would continue using the processes after our partnership was officially over. Powerful dialogue and discussions occurred between and among teams. For example, when examining interim data across the district, it was discovered that the junior high school didn't have items on the benchmark assessment that measured its GAN. That omission was quickly corrected. Schools shared how they were making sense of each of the main components of the SMART goals process, and the sharing of implementation strategies built a web across the district. Schools were able to share

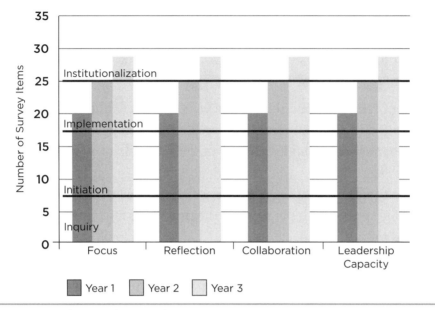

Figure 5.4: Implementation over time.

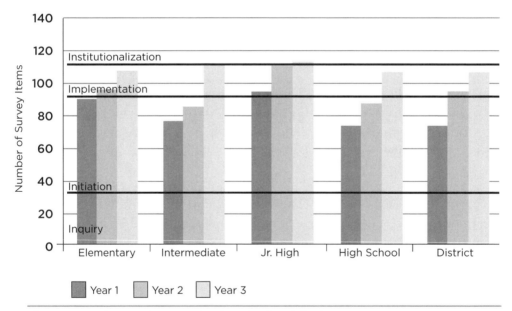

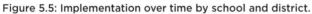

Figure 5.5: Implementation over time by school and district.

strategies to address variations in the functioning levels of their teams.

With the steering committee, we looked at the process, technical advice, relationships, and strategies, always seating the discussion in whether what we were doing was getting results for students. While the steering committee was comprised of the lead implementers, they were asked to step out of their roles of principal, teacher, director of curriculum and professional development, and superintendent and think as representatives of the whole district.

Simultaneously, the school leadership teams were deepening their understanding of how to implement the process within their classrooms through coaching. Teachers started collaborating as grade-level teams, analyzing themselves against the IoP. The teams offered evidence of their growth, which was then shared at the district level through the steering committee for the purpose of recommending what would strengthen the work. On the other hand, when one grade-level team allowed its dysfunction to impact student improvement, it became obvious and could be addressed. Over time, it became clear that perspectives had changed, that each school and the whole system could see itself as part of a preK–12 spectrum.

CHAPTER 6

Engaging the Mind, Body, and Spirit

Never lie to your horse.

—CHRIS COX

There is an emerging philosophy about the relationship between humans and horses called *joining up*. Once thought to be one of master and servant, the relationship is now viewed as a partnership.

At a recent joining-up clinic for horse owners, Anne watched a gentle cowboy work magic with one feisty steed after another. He began by removing some of the constraining equipment that has traditionally been used to control the horse. This was perplexing for the owners. After all, they had come to the clinic because they had been ineffective in controlling their horses; to remove the only control mechanisms they had seemed odd, if not dangerous.

The next step was to get the horse to move with the cowboy, not away from him. He gave the horse a gentle nudge in just the right place to signal the horse to move in one direction or another. Most people try to move a horse by pulling on the reins and halter. But the horse is bigger and stronger than the human, and when he decides he's not going to move, jerking his head is only going to make him mad. The cowboy told the gathered owners that the day he realized that he had to work with the whole animal—body, spirit, and mind—was the day he became an effective horseman. He went on to say that, as the owner, you've got to work with the horse, get him to move by engaging his body, and then build a relationship by engaging his mind and spirit.

As the cowboy worked, he explained every move he made and predicted every move the horse would make. Frequently, he would interject, "Never lie to your horse." He meant that you have to be consistent. When you encourage the horse to go in one direction, don't punish him for going there. When you want the horse to come to you, don't jerk on his head—to the horse, that's a punishment. The horse learns that you are not consistent with your messages, that you can't be trusted. Trust building is the essence of the relationship that brings man and horse into partnership with one another.

Many of the lessons learned at this clinic translate to working in schools. Some of the lessons are obvious, others more subtle. When it comes to joining up, three stand out:

1. The value of removing constraints while providing direction through the use of subtle methods and supportive actions and words

2. The importance of being consistent in the messages we give and the actions we take

3. The importance of building relationships and trust by engaging the whole being—body, mind, and spirit

The Nudge

Simple logic tells us that if we want something to happen in a particular way, we need to exercise a certain amount of control over the situation. Simple logic also tells us that if we want to head in a particular direction, then we need to be out in front, leading and moving in that direction. Based on the lessons learned in joining up, neither of these simple truths is accurate. In fact, there's nothing simple or logical about them. We have explored the nature of systems change. The inherent complexities of moving a human system require a much deeper understanding of the interdependence of the various parts of the system as well as knowledge about the profound impact of the dynamics of human engagement within those systems.

The counterintuitive message about both control (remove the constraints) and movement (engage the horse by pushing in the opposite direction that you want the horse to move) is similar to Buckminster Fuller's concept of leverage as an analogy for leading systemic change (as cited in Senge, 1990). High-leverage changes in human systems are typically *not obvious*. Fuller uses the *trim tab* as his example:

> A trim tab is a small rudder on the rudder of a ship. It is only a fraction the size of the rudder. Its function is to make it easier to turn the rudder, which, then, makes it easier to turn the ship. . . .

> If you knew absolutely nothing about hydrodynamics and you saw a large oil tanker plowing through the high seas, where would you push if you wanted the tanker to turn left? . . . The leverage lies in going to the stern (back of the ship) and pushing the tail end of the tanker to the right, in order to turn the front to the left. This, of course, is the job of the rudder. But in what direction does the rudder turn in order to get the ship's stern to turn to the right? Why to the left, of course.
>
> You see, ships turn because their stern is "sucked around." . . . The trim tab—this very small device that has an enormous effect on the huge ship—does the same for the rudder. . . . If you want the rudder to turn to the left, what direction do you turn the trim tab? To the right, naturally. (as cited in Senge, 1990, pp. 64–65)

The best actions for moving the system may not be obvious because they are usually not close in time and space to the occurrence of the problem. An example of this would be the traditional model for professional development. Most would agree that professional development is an effective practice for promoting improvement. However, because professional development is traditionally separated in time (for example, designated days in the year, summers, or Saturdays) and space (for example, off-campus, local or distant hotels, or universities), the connection between what is being learned and the intended applications gets lost.

The recent move toward goal-driven, school-based professional learning closes the time and space gap. It directly connects the new learning to the need and the application, thereby strengthening the implementation and impact of the new learning and increasing the probability that the new learning will result in better outcomes for students. Making the shift to this new model, as logical as it seems, has been arduous, not because it has been resisted per se, but because the entire existing system is comprised of underlying, countervailing structures that are also not obvious (for example, norms and values, contractual agreements, policies, schedules, organizational structures, performance management practices, and so on). If we do not understand the system structures that are at play and do not do the hard work of analyzing what is not obvious, we will continue to employ low-leverage, event-driven solutions to address deep-rooted, structural problems. These *solutions* actually throw the system into greater instability, leading to unpredictable outcomes and random, desperate attempts at improvement. Hence the pandemonium created by a multitude of level I initiatives.

The concept of leverage is all about using small, well-focused actions to produce significant results. Just as a gentle nudge is all that is needed to turn a 1,200-pound animal, and a small strategically located trim tab is what is needed to turn a massive oil tanker, a few well-timed and simple leadership actions can make an enormous difference in the implementation of significant improvement efforts. The following guidelines illustrate the leadership actions described in our first lesson of horsemanship. We have tapped Richard Elmore's (2000) work for the theory and our practitioners for the examples.

Commit to One High-Leverage Strategy That Is Likely to Have the Greatest Impact

The principal of a Phoenix-area elementary school confided that his high-leverage strategy for change is a little like chasing butterflies. He sees multiple, connected initiatives for improvement as a field full of beautiful butterflies in motion. His challenge, as a leader, is to catch the one that has the greatest promise and stay with it. The butterfly he has captured is called PLCs. Side by side, he and his teacher leaders cultivate a rich learning environment through dialogue, professional learning, and active engagement in the work of leading change. PLCs are their primary vehicle for the change process. Improving instruction is their primary focus; improving student learning is their primary goal. Much is happening, but it's all connected to one ultimate aim.

When we urge you to find a single strategy, we're not suggesting that improvement is as simple as doing one thing. Redesigning school structures and improving professional practice are enormously complex endeavors. They "involve changes of the most fundamental kind in the norms and values that shape work in schools, in the way the resources of the system get used, in the skills and knowledge that people bring to their work, and in how people relate to each other around the work of the organization" (Elmore, 2000, p. 26). These are not single tasks that can be checked off a to-do list. They are interwoven in a complex fabric of human dynamics.

Stay Focused on Getting Your High-Leverage Strategy Fully Implemented

Based on our field research, we assert that staying the course is probably the greatest challenge facing educators today. Too many change efforts are begun and then abandoned before they are fully implemented and their impact fully realized. Elmore (2000) suggests that large-scale improvement is really about collective problem solving, which requires a certain level of sophistication about the learning process: "Learning about improvement occurs in growth and development of common understandings about why things happen the way they do" (p. 13). It takes time for this growth to occur because it involves people engaging in conversations that they've never had before. Significant change doesn't happen overnight. Using an intentional and steady approach that maintains a focus on the chosen strategy and keeps actions (research, dialogue, implementation, and monitoring) directed toward the ultimate goal is what will result in more significant and lasting improvements. As people learn how to learn in community, they will develop skills and confidence in implementing the process, all of which will build ownership of and commitment to the change.

One example of staying focused on a high-level strategy comes from a principal newly assigned to a veteran staff in an elementary school in the Midwest. This principal hadn't been in the building more than a month before she recognized that reform wasn't going to be a quick or easy sell. She used sustained, embedded professional development as her high-leverage strategy for introducing data, building collaborative teams, setting goals, and studying best practices for improving student learning. She built a long-term model that was based on individual staff needs and preferences. She created a survey that she used at the beginning of each year to determine what teachers needed to learn and how they wanted to learn. Over the years, the staff engaged in a variety of learning strategies—peer coaching, study teams, videos, and both on-site and off-site workshops and conferences. They were expected to share their learning with their colleagues through internal workshops, classroom modeling and observations, and peer collaboration teams. The payoff was slow but steady progress, exhibited by consistently improved results in student learning (Abplanalp, 2007).

Continuously Monitor Both the Change Process and Its Effects on Student Learning

Feedback from the continuous evaluation and monitoring of the change process is needed to make adjustments along the way. Elmore (2000) notes that educators tend to proclaim victory based on their individual perceptions that a change has been successful because they have altered their practice in some way. However, they may not have clear evidence that students actually know and are able to do things they haven't previously known or done. Such a scenario "produces lots of change and not much improvement" (Elmore, 2000, p. 12). Instead, we need to think about how we can systematically gather evidence connected to our improvement strategy. According to Elmore (2000), "a major source of learning in such situations is analysis and discussion of successes and failures, and feedback about this into the larger pool of knowledge and skill in the organization" (p. 13).

In a Wisconsin school district, the principals have teamed up to coordinate the districtwide implementation of the SMART goals process as their systemic improvement strategy. Led by school-based leadership teams of teachers from all grade levels and departments, the district made a three-year commitment to get everyone on board with the process. They use SMS to keep their collective finger on the pulse of change and to monitor ongoing student results via their multifaceted benchmark, formative, and summative assessment system.

Give Permission for the Process to Be Messy

According to Elmore (2000), "improvement seldom, if ever, occurs on a straight trajectory; it typically involves bumps and slides, as well as gratifying leaps" (p. 13). The important thing is to embed a means for learning from the bumps, slides, and leaps along the way, which requires a resiliency that is uncharacteristic in contemporary school systems. Traditional leadership takes an opposite approach, seeking to keep things orderly, predictable, and under control. Remember our horsemanship lesson about removing constraints to compel movement. To lead change is to guide and direct change, not control it.

Since most of the knowledge required for improvement is generated by the act of instruction, those who deliver instruction are those who must direct the change. For this to happen, it is imperative that teachers have the freedom and the permission to explore new ideas and, yes, even to fail—and that can get messy. Loosening control can be a scary proposition for many leaders. We are not advocating anarchy or reckless abandonment of order, nor are we suggesting that there not be clear standards that are adhered to by all. There are clearly things that will always require control and should not be considered voluntary or by invitation only (DuFour, 2007; Elmore, 2000). But, in the name of instructional improvement, general parameters, clear direction, guidance, support, and permission to fail forward are better alternatives than tightly held reins.

In one high-performing school district in Illinois, getting staff to buy into a reform agenda was anything but a cakewalk. Knowing that, the superintendent used baking a cake as his analogy for the change process. He told his staff, "It's going to be messy at first. Eggs will break, flour will be all over the place, but that's all part of the process." This kind of message gives people permission to experiment, test ideas, and even do some things that might not work. The conversations in this district moved from predictable questioning to dogged determination in pursuit of getting better results for the students. Apparently, one can have one's cake and eat it, too.

Help People See How the Initiative Connects to and Enhances Current Improvement Work

At some point in our lives, we've all been deeply immersed in dealing with the parts of something and thus unable to see the whole. Our traditional organizational structures and methods of work distribution in education require compartmentalization with an almost maniacal focus on only the parts. It's very difficult for those working in the system to see the big picture.

In one of our client districts in Texas, school-based leadership teams were asked to identify all of the initiatives they were a part of that directly affected their classroom practice. Using a Venn diagram for which the three spheres were labeled *curriculum*, *instruction*, and *professional development*, the teams quickly got to work recording the various initiatives. Where initiatives addressed more than one of the spheres, they put them in the overlapping areas of the diagram. This helped them see the interrelationship of the parts; it also helped to create clarity about why each initiative was important to the whole. When they were finished mapping, we connected the disparate initiatives and gave direction and focus to what had initially been deemed random acts of improvement.

There are many different ways to help people see and commit to the big picture but none as powerful as engaging people in the process of defining organizational goals. Elmore (2000) tells us, "Organizations that improve do so because they create and nurture agreement on what is worth achieving and they set in motion the internal processes by which people progressively learn how to do what they need to do in order to achieve what is worthwhile"

(p. 25). The act of exploring and examining professional practices in targeted areas where data have revealed significant achievement gaps creates connections between theory and practice at progressively deeper levels. Elmore (2000) refers to this as social learning. It connects people with each other and to new ideas. Those ideas then become scrutinized, measured against organizational goals, and tested in practice. This is the work of PLCs. This is how organizations learn.

Participate Fully as a Co-Learner and Co-Leader of the Process

Reciprocity in accountability is inherent in a co-leader and co-learner relationship. Elmore (2000) suggests, "If anyone's practice is subject to observation, analysis, and critique, then everyone's practice should be. The principle of reciprocity applies to all accountability relationships; there can be no demands without attention to the capacity that exists to deliver them" (p. 32).

Susan Abplanalp (2007) believes that the learning leader, one who learns along with her staff and colleagues, more deeply understands the impact of the learning from the perspective of those who must translate it into practice. Therefore, the learning leader is more likely not to introduce something the system doesn't have the capacity to carry out.

As an example of co-leaders and co-learners, we return to our Illinois district where the superintendent, his central office leaders, and all of the principals are fully present with their teacher leadership teams throughout the learning process—not once, but for every possible opportunity. They participate in the activities, listen to their staff, offer their perspectives without judgment, and share their own hopes and fears about what they are learning. They are there as learners as much as they are there as leaders.

The involvement of administrators as learning leaders doesn't represent a dramatic change in terms of daily routine, but its impact is not lost on the teachers. One teacher described the difference: "It used to be that the principals would go off and learn something and then come back and just tell us what to do. That was nice in one respect, but it didn't do anything to build community. Now they're learning right beside us. It's a different feeling, a more professional feeling."

An Arizona principal shares the same philosophy. Through all phases of his four-part professional development strategy, he accompanies teams of teachers as they learn about critical aspects of becoming effective PLCs—collaboration, common assessments, SMART goals, and pyramid response to intervention. His role is to support the learning teams by providing time and opportunities to share what they are learning with the rest of the staff. As the architect of the plan, this principal orchestrates the flow of learning and helps people connect the dots. If he weren't an active learner along with the teams, his ability to provide appropriate support and to coordinate the capacity-building process would be limited.

Do as I Say and as I Do

The second lesson of horsemanship dealt with consistency between what is said and what is done. When there is a perceived lack of congruence between the leader's words and actions, trust is eroded. Never lie to your horse.

More often than not, leaders have high levels of integrity and are very sincere in both their words and their actions. But the perception is sometimes that when times get tough, decisions are based on politics, budgets, or pressures from above, not on the espoused or stated values, goals, or priorities of the leader or the school. As our cowboy reminds us, "Whatever you do, be consistent. Mixed signals lead to confusion and then resentment. You must be the same in the saddle as you are on the ground" (Cox, 2011).

Consistency is both an internal and an external phenomenon. It begins internally with the leader being clear about his personal values, goals, and priorities and is manifest externally by how he acts in relation to those values, goals, and priorities. Kris Hipp, professor in doctoral leadership studies, begins the three-year doctoral and district administrator licensure programs at Cardinal Stritch University with a course that focuses on leading self. In it, she asks her students to reflect on and write about these questions:

- What do I value?
- To what extent am I *living* my stated values?
- Do I believe that I can make a difference?
- What is my moral purpose, and what am I doing to achieve it?
- What legacy do I want to leave?
- How am I spending my time?

These questions get deeply at the real priorities that drive individuals to behave the way they do. They reveal aspirations and beliefs about one's purpose in life. Since leaders bring life to leadership, aspirations and beliefs are pretty important aspects of the decisions leaders make and the actions they take on behalf of those they lead and serve (Hipp & Huffman, 2010).

Reflecting on who we are, what we value, and what we bring to our life's work is at the foundation of becoming an effective leader. Self-reflection leads to personal mastery, one of five disciplines that Peter Senge writes about in his seminal work *The Fifth Discipline: The Art and Practice of the Learning Organization*. Senge (1990) defines personal mastery as "the discipline of personal growth and learning" and then goes on to state that "people with high levels of personal mastery are continually expanding their ability to create the results in life they truly seek" (p. 141).

Developing personal mastery is itself a reflective practice—a discipline—something we integrate into our daily lives. It is more than the development of skills and competencies, although that is certainly an important element. Personal mastery is a continual interplay between knowing what is truly important and examining the current reality in relation to that goal or vision. Through ongoing reflection, learning, and clarification within these two realms, we are able to create new realities that are consistent with our values. Senge refers to this dynamic as *creative tension*. Creative tension is "the force that comes into play at the moment when we acknowledge a vision that is at odds with current reality" (Senge, 1990, p. 151).

Let's examine how that looks inside the walls of a school. As a teacher, I value students who demonstrate motivation for learning, who apply themselves fully to their studies, and who work well with others in my classroom. As a principal, I value staff members who demonstrate motivation for their work, who apply themselves fully to their jobs, and who work well with others in my school. The logic continues as you move up and out from the school. If these are the things we value, how do they measure up with what is currently happening? If the reality is inconsistent with what is valued, then tension exists, not just for the principal or the teachers, but for the students and parents as well. As the saying goes, actions speak louder than words, so when others witness actions that are not consistent with what they are told, they will believe what they see. This is a pivotal point of opportunity for leadership. Do you focus on the reality and try to fix it, or do you focus on the vision and try to create it? Effective leaders do both.

The first order of business is looking critically at one's own behaviors in relation to the stated values. How am I contributing to the current reality? How am I not contributing to the preferred reality? Am I clear about what I truly want? What is my personal vision? Am I committed to making it happen? If the leader can't answer these questions, it is difficult, if not impossible, to act in ways that are perceived to be consistent. Furthermore, how can he or she expect others within the organization to follow suit? Fixing the current reality and creating the preferred reality starts with personal mastery.

As creative tension is a by-product of engaging the faculty in creating goals designed to close the gap between vision and reality, it is actually a good thing, providing the motivation and energy for closing that gap. The very act of engaging the faculty is a high-leverage strategy for bringing consistency and meaning to any change effort.

Trust Me, I'm the Leader

Our third lesson of horsemanship speaks to the importance of trust and engagement in building relationships. Trust is difficult to measure, but we all seem to know when it's there and when it's not. It is even more difficult to sustain. Trust can be fleeting and is almost always at risk somewhere in the organization. When a school or district is experiencing conflict or resistance to change, issues of trust are inevitably at the core of the problem. The leader is frequently perplexed by the lack of trust because he or she has not knowingly done anything that would be considered untrustworthy. But that's not really what it's about. Yes, a single act that might be perceived as deceitful, disloyal, or dishonest will most certainly lead to the belief that this is a person who cannot be trusted. However, when we talk about the kind of trust that is needed to build and sustain relationships characteristic of high-performance cultures, we're talking about a proactive investment of time engaging in very deliberate interactions. Trust building is an ongoing, intentional, and active process.

The key to leadership is building relationships in which people *choose to join* the journey—and that requires trust. We once heard a superintendent say to his principals, "You're not the principal until your staff and parents choose you as their principal." Of course, these days, there's often a committee of staff and parents who participate in the selection process when hiring a new principal, but that's not what he meant. New principals frequently assume that because they are given the official position and title, they are, therefore, the principal. The philosophy of this superintendent was that, until trust has been established, anyone in the role of principal is there in name only. Unless a mutually respectful relationship develops, in which people *choose to join* the journey, the leader in name is destined to spend his or her precious time and energy pulling hard against a much stronger force.

There is a growing body of research that supports this philosophy. Anthony Bryk and Barbara Schneider (2003) conducted a longitudinal analysis of case study research on more than four hundred elementary schools in Chicago. Additionally, they analyzed surveys completed by teachers, principals, and students over a six-year period and identified trends in student reading and math achievement. Their findings were impressive:

> Elementary schools with high relational trust were much more likely to demonstrate marked improvements in student learning. Our overall measure of school trust . . . proved a powerful discriminator between improving and non-improving schools. On average, improving schools recorded increases in student learning of 8 percent in reading and 20 percent in mathematics in a five-year period. The schools in the non-improving group lost ground in reading and stayed about the same in mathematics. Most significant was the finding that schools with chronically weak trust reports throughout the period of study had virtually no chance of improving in either reading or mathematics. (Bryk & Schneider, 2003, p. 43)

The researchers went on to explain their results. In matters of school improvement, broad-based buy-in on the part of teachers is critical for reform. Collective decision making through the active engagement of staff is more likely to be the norm in schools with strong relational trust. Because improvement requires a certain amount of risk taking, trust becomes the "connecting tissue that holds the schools together" (Aguilar, 2011). According to Bryk and Schneider (2003), "in schools where relational trust was improving over time, teachers increasingly characterized their colleagues as committed and loyal to the school and more eager to engage in new practices that might help students learn better" (p. 43).

It is the job of leadership to create a culture in which every individual can trust and be trusted. As one principal so beautifully stated, "For every act of trust we extend to one another, the child reaps the benefits" (as cited in Conzemius & O'Neill, 1998). With so much at stake for our students, we can't afford not to pay attention to our relationships as adults.

What are the behaviors that build and sustain trust? The following are responses from teachers when asked what they need from their leaders:

- I need to know I'm safe—I can trust that my confidence will be kept, that I am respected, and that I will not be chastised for my point of view.

- I need to know that I can successfully fail at something new, learn from it, and go on.

- I need to know that what we are doing is in the best interest of my students and that the hard work will pay off in terms of better learning outcomes.

- I need honesty, consistency, and direct, specific feedback delivered with sensitivity.

- I need someone who really listens—beyond the words—listens in order to understand.

- I need follow-through and thoroughness.

- I need support.

Note that this isn't a list that is unique to teachers and principals. Look at the list again, this time while thinking of any person with whom you have a significant relationship—a spouse or partner, your parents or children, your clergy or neighbor. It is a list of expectations that we should have for everyone in our lives, including ourselves.

Personal and interpersonal qualities that contribute to trust are:

1. Character

2. Competence

3. Caring

4. Commitment

Of the four, *character* is the most fundamental and most taken for granted. Character is who we are. It is manifest in principled behaviors such as unselfishness, self-control, and respect for our fellow human beings. When we have character, we have the ability to give and forgive. When character is in question, we lose the power to influence and, hence, to lead.

Competence is not a quality that people often attach to trust. But when you think about why you trust your life to your surgeon or the pilot in the cockpit of the plane you just boarded, it comes down to believing that they are competent and that they have continued to increase their knowledge about their professional practice since first being licensed. An important part of creating a culture of trust is encouraging the professional growth that promotes increasing levels of competence and understanding. The leader should ask:

- Do I value my own professional growth, improvement, and continual learning?
- Do I value the professional growth, improvement, and continual learning of others?

Caring means that we are genuinely concerned about the well-being of others. There is no question that educators care deeply about the children. They wouldn't be in the profession if that were not true. But caring for each other isn't always so evident. In the hustle and bustle of our busy lives, we forget to show how much we care. Leaders should actively pursue opportunities to express and recognize acts of caring among adults as well as among the children.

When all is said and done, knowing and believing are not doing. Commitment requires action. The doing part of leadership is just plain hard work. It is work that *we will not do* if we do not care about its importance or are not competent. It is work that *we cannot do* if we lack the character. It is work that extends beyond every other piece of work that we do to keep the place running, and it is work that will never end. Commitment to the mission, commitment to the values, and commitment to the people is what trustworthy leadership is all about.

When these are the prevailing qualities demonstrated in an organization, people come together in community in ways that are not otherwise possible. There is no limit to what can be accomplished when trust permeates the culture.

Tools and Processes for Joining Up

Back to our horse story. Our cowboy became truly effective when he realized that he needed to engage the whole animal. He said that you've got to work *with* the horse, get him to move by engaging his body, and then build a relationship by engaging his mind and spirit. When we engage body, mind, and spirit, we acknowledge the wholeness of what the animal brings to the process of joining up. The cowboy knows that this is how relationships are built, particularly when there is either a natural resistance that needs to be overcome (there's nothing natural about having a human on your back) or if the task that is being required is new, unknown, or perceived to be a threat to one's survival (until otherwise trained, horses view people as predators). Much like the Chinese proverb "Tell me and I'll forget; show me and I may remember; involve me and I'll understand," the more we can fully engage people in examining the very thing that frightens them, the more deeply they will understand and ultimately commit to joining up.

For example, data is an important feedback mechanism for improvement. For some, the resistance to using data is rooted in fear of the unknown. After all, this is not an area of expertise that educators have traditionally explored, and it doesn't feel the least bit natural. For others, resistance has more to do with fear of being exposed as less than competent or attacked by the media, parents, or fellow staff members. Adding to the uncertainty is the expectation that school and team goals will be based on data and that they may become part of a broader accountability system that determines one's fate or compensation. Using data and goal setting for accountability requires a safe context, and building trust is vital to creating that context.

When we introduce the use of data for the first time, we ask people to talk about their concerns. Getting those concerns out on the table at the beginning sends the message that we know data can be threatening and that we want to do whatever we can to reduce the anxiety associated with looking at the data in the presence of others. We use a lighthearted approach borrowed from our friend Maury Cotter, director of the Office of Quality Improvement at the University of Wisconsin–Madison. She begins meetings with new groups by asking them to identify what they could do to assure that their time together will be a complete disaster. Usually the reaction includes knowing expressions and a few chuckles from the group members. They've been there, done that, and now they get to name it. From their list of potential disasters, they develop agreements on what they will do to make sure those things don't happen. Specifically, when it comes to examining data, we ask teams to create a T-chart on a piece of chart paper and label the two columns *Disaster* and *Trust Rule*. We then give them several minutes to brainstorm all the things they can think of that could make the use of data in their school a disaster (no names, please). There are always plenty of ideas to fill the paper. After a brief discussion to clarify and consolidate the ideas, the team selects its top three to five disasters and writes a set of trust rules for avoiding them. No one is singled out, and everyone has the opportunity to participate in defining the norms of a data-driven culture. This is just one simple example of how easily the minds, bodies, and spirits of people can be engaged in building trust and commitment to change.

Another process that results in more profound commitment to joining up is a special type of communication called *dialogue*. Dialogue is a tool for addressing what Senge (1990) refers to as mental modes, "deeply ingrained assumptions, generalizations, or even pictures of how we understand the world" (p. 8). Mental models shape the dialogue process. They influence the way we think about things, what we pay attention to, and ultimately what we choose to do about whatever it is that we are seeing and hearing. Resistance is often the result of strong mental models that have been shaped over time; we may not even be aware of them as we go about our daily routines. As an example, some of us believe that we are doing our best to teach and that we have been successful in helping students learn. Our mental model about the system in which we teach is that it is perfectly fine the way it is, since, until recently, it hasn't been our practice to look for evidence that would suggest otherwise. We are content to continue down the path that has shaped the mental model that leads us to think that we don't have a problem. So when we hear from the media that there's a crisis in education, we filter out that information. What we hear instead is that other schools are in crisis—they're not talking about us; they're talking about the school down the road or in another part of the country. That leads us to conclude that we don't need to change. When we are presented with data that are contrary to our prevailing mental model, we may not even be able to see them. We have to be able to look at the data differently to confront our habitual way of thinking about our students and their learning. Mental models aren't necessarily bad or wrong. However, being aware of them and understanding them can help us change them and our behaviors associated with them if we choose.

The use of dialogue generally as a tool for promoting understanding and creating meaning is a high-leverage strategy for building trust and strengthening relationships. The word *dialogue* is derived from two Latin root words, *dia* and *logos*, which together mean "creating meaning through words." The process of dialogue is a give-and-take, or a balancing act—the balance between telling people what we think (advocacy) and hearing what they think (inquiry). It's being open to sharing and challenging the underlying assumptions that lead us to think the way we do and then comparing those assumptions with those of others. Open exploration of ideas is at the root of effective dialogue. It fuels what Lambert (1998) refers to as reciprocal learning, wherein listening to others is as much a part of the equation as telling others what you know. Use of the following guidelines will assure that dialogue gets to deep understanding:

- Speak from your personal point of view. Since the purpose of dialogue is to seek meaning and understanding, it's important that participants speak from their own perspectives. One doesn't have to be an expert or even know what the experts think or know. It's all about what the individuals who are having the dialogue think about the issue, question, or data being explored.

- Replace seeking resolution with living in and working through the question. Be open to wondering together. It's OK if the group doesn't resolve the issue immediately. Use "what if?" statements to prod deeper before trying to find an answer or solution.

- Allow each person time and space to reflect. This is what makes dialogue feel so different from a casual conversation, and sometimes uncomfortable. You'll find that it moves more slowly and that there's more dead air that is not filled with someone's voice as people are being allowed to process and learn from others' information and think through their own understanding. Reflection time is an important characteristic of dialogue.

- Listen for and identify underlying assumptions. When someone is talking, listen for meaning behind the words. Ask the person to share the basis of his or her thinking. If you're talking, share the assumptions that led you to the conclusion or meaning that you are sharing. For example: "I think the data show that we have a problem serving the needs of our poorest children. I'm assuming that those on the lowest end are the kids who either come from another district or are from the Jamestown neighborhood." This allows others to understand your thinking and be able to ask why you are making the assumptions that you do, which, in turn, will most likely lead you to question your own assumptions.

- View disagreement as an opportunity to learn and a sign that this is a place to dig deeper. In the example we just gave, another person in the group might have looked at the data or situation differently: "I saw it another way. We're not sure who these kids are, but even if they are poor, what's our responsibility for making sure they have what they need to succeed? How can we know better what the needs are of the lowest quartile, regardless of their economic or educational history?" This disagreement leads to a deeper or different understanding.

- Remain self-aware so that you can consciously use your feelings and perceptions as a resource. Every once in a while, step outside your own head and view what's happening in the group as a whole. This is called metacognition; it helps you be more aware of how you are participating and responding to the dialogue.

- Respect different points of view as every bit as valid as your own. There are no experts here, just people who want to learn together and from each other. Be open to the fact that your point of view is just that—yours. And others' points of view are just that—theirs. Now try to understand why you have such different points of view. That's where the real, reciprocal learning takes place.

These guidelines for dialogue are important precursors to any conversation during which people may feel vulnerable or exposed. For example, when SMART goals have been set based on team and classroom data, there is a direct relationship between what is being taught, how it is being taught, and the results that are being achieved. This is a very personal matter for teachers. If trust has not been intentionally cultivated, the likelihood that instructional change will voluntarily occur is pretty slim. What can leaders do to create the environment for improvement? Once again, engaging the mind, body, and spirit of every teacher is at the core of the answer. But it must go beyond trust-building activities to the level of commitment. It is important that the teachers themselves identify what they are willing to commit to in highly specific behavioral terms. We suggest the use of the Affinity Process (see Conzemius & O'Neill, 2002, pp. 90–91) as a good starting point. The process begins with a brainstormed response to the question, What promises are we willing to make to each other to assure our collective success? Similar ideas are grouped, prioritized, and then translated into statements of observable behaviors that reflect the collective commitments of the entire staff. By creating statements of observable behaviors, the faculty is making a public statement about what it values. The actions that are taken or the behaviors that are exhibited can be measured against those standards. This creates accountability for maintaining consistency between what is said and what is done on the part of everyone in the school.

Communication is the key to building the trust that is needed to lead and learn in community and to sustaining the trust that is earned. Constant communication in a variety of forms and venues will do more to build and sustain trust than just about anything else leaders can do. In our horse story, the cowboy never lost communication with his horse. He talked to the horse, petted him, rewarded him, or nudged him the entire time he worked, and the horse communicated back through his actions and inactions. The two were engaged in a continuous cycle of communication. Joining up is a reciprocal learning process that is sustained by communication in a trusting and mutually respectful environment.

On a final note, Anne recently had an opportunity to try out the joining-up process when one of the horses on the family ranch left the pasture in pursuit of greener grass. With the ranch hands either occupied or off the property, it was time to put her learning to the test. Slowly, she approached the animal, speaking to him in calm and steady terms of endearment until she was at his side. The horse looked up and then away toward the pasture, seeming to know where he was destined to go. Without a hint of resistance, he dutifully allowed himself to be led back inside the fence. It didn't hurt that a fresh flake of hay awaited his return.

REFERENCES

Abplanalp, S. L. (2007). *Breaking the low-achieving mindset: A SMART journey of purposeful change.* Madison, WI: QLD Learning.

Aguilar, E. (2011). How teachers can build emotional resilience. *Education Week Teacher.* Accessed at www.edweek.org/tm/articles/2011/01/05/tln_resilience.html on March 17, 2011.

Battle, D., & Gruber, K. (2010). *Principal attrition and mobility: Results from the 2008–09 principal follow-up survey.* Washington, DC: Institute of Education Sciences, National Center for Education Statistics.

Black, P., & Wiliam, D. (1998). Inside the black box: Raising standards through classroom assessment. *Phi Delta Kappan, 80*(2), 139–148.

Block, P. (2008). *Community: The structure of belonging.* San Francisco: Berrett-Koehler.

Bryk, A. S., & Schneider, B. (2003). Trust in schools: A core resource for school reform. *Educational Leadership, 60*(6), 40–45.

Buffum, A., Mattos, M., & Weber, C. (2009). *Pyramid response to intervention: RTI, professional learning communities, and how to respond when kids don't learn.* Bloomington, IN: Solution Tree Press.

Chilcott, L. (Producer), & Guggenheim, D. (Director). (2010). *Waiting for "Superman"* [Motion picture]. United States: Paramount Pictures.

Christensen, C. M., Horn, M. B., & Johnson, C. W. (2008). *Disrupting class: How disruptive innovation will change the way the world learns.* New York: McGraw Hill.

Conzemius, A. (2010). A minimalist approach to reform: A smart, sane and strategic route focuses principals and teachers on fewer high priorities. *The School Administrator, 67*(1), 32–36.

Conzemius, A., & O'Neill, J. (1998). *Creating meaning through measurement: How our school got SMART about accountability* [Video]. Madison, WI: QLD Learning.

Conzemius, A., & O'Neill, J. (2002). *The handbook for SMART school teams.* Bloomington, IN: Solution Tree Press.

Costa, A. L. (2006). Foreword. In J. York-Barr, W. A. Sommers, G. S. Ghere, & J. Montie (Eds.), *Reflective practice to improve schools: An action guide for educators* (pp. xv–xviii). Thousand Oaks, CA: Corwin Press.

Covey, S. R. (1989). *The 7 habits of highly effective people.* New York: Simon and Schuster.

Covey, S. R. (1994). *First things first.* New York: Simon and Schuster.

Cox, C. (2011). Training philosophy 101. Accessed at www.chris-cox.com /101.shtml on March 15, 2011.

Csikszentmihalyi, M. (1990). *Flow: The psychology of optimal experience.* New York: Harper and Row.

Damon, W. (2008). The moral north star. *Educational Leadership, 66*(2), 8–12.

Darling-Hammond, L. (2008). Target time towards teachers. In V. von Frank (Ed.), *Finding time for professional learning* (p. 6). Dallas, TX: National Staff Development Council.

Darling-Hammond, L., Wei, R. C., Andree, A., Richardson, N., & Orphanos, S. (2009). *Professional learning in the learning profession: A status report on teacher development in the United States and abroad.* Dallas, TX: National Staff Development Council.

Davidovich, R., Nikolay, P., Laugerman, B., & Commodore, C. (2010). *Beyond school improvement: The journey to innovative leadership.* Thousand Oaks, CA: Corwin Press.

Deming, W. E. (1986). *Out of the crisis.* Boston: MIT Press.

Deming, W. E. (1993). *The new economics for industry, government, education* (2nd ed.). Boston: MIT Press.

Deutsch, M. (1962). Cooperation and trust: Some theoretical notes. In M. R. Jones (Ed.), *Nebraska symposium on motivation* (pp. 275–319). Lincoln: University of Nebraska Press.

Dolan, W. P. (1994). *Restructuring our schools: A primer on systemic change.* Kansas City, MO: Systems and Organization.

DuFour, R. (2007). In praise of top-down leadership. *The School Administrator, 64*(10), 38–42.

DuFour, R., & Eaker, R. (1998). *Professional learning communities at work: Best practices for enhancing student achievement.* Bloomington, IN: Solution Tree Press.

Eastman, L. B. (Ed.). (2008). *Powerful designs for professional learning* (2nd ed.). Oxford, OH: National Staff Development Council.

Education Trust. (2010). Closing the gaps. Accessed at www.edtrust.org /issues/pre-k-12/closing-the-gaps on March 17, 2011.

Elmore, R. F. (2000). *Building a new structure for school leadership.* Washington, DC: The Albert Shanker Institute. Accessed at www .shankerinstitute.org/Downloads/building.pdf on March 17, 2011.

Flippen Group. (2010). Capturing kids' hearts. Accessed at www .flippengroup.com/education/ckh.html on March 17, 2011.

Frank, L. S. (2001). *The caring classroom: Using adventure to create community in the classroom and beyond.* Madison, WI: GOAL Consulting.

Fullan, M. G. (1991). *The new meaning of educational change.* New York: Teachers College Press.

Fullan, M. G. (2010). *Motion leadership: The skinny on becoming change savvy.* Thousand Oaks, CA: Corwin Press.

Gardner, H. (1993). *Frames of mind: The theory of multiple intelligences.* New York: Basic Books.

Garmston, R. J., & Wellman, B. M. (1999). *The adaptive school: A sourcebook for developing collaborative groups.* Norwood, MA: Christopher-Gordon.

Gibbs, J. (1995). *Tribes: A new way of learning and being together.* Sausalito,

CA: CenterSource Systems.

Guskey, T. R. (2000). *Evaluating professional development.* Thousand Oaks, CA: Corwin Press.

Hall, G. E., & Hord, S. M. (2011). *Implementing change: Patterns, principles, and potholes* (3rd ed.). Upper Saddle River, NJ: Pearson Education.

Hipp, K. K., & Huffman, J. B. (Eds.). (2010). *Demystifying professional learning communities: School leadership at its best.* Lanham, MD: Rowman & Littlefield.

Hirsh, S., & Killion, J. (2008). *The learning educator: A new era for professional learning.* Oxford, OH: National Staff Development Council.

Hord, S. M. (1997). *Professional learning communities: Communities of continuous inquiry and improvement.* (Eric Document Reproduction Service No. ED 410659) Austin, TX: Southwest Educational Development Laboratory.

Hord, S. M., Roussin, J. L., & Sommers, W. A. (2010). *Guiding professional learning communities: Inspiration, challenge, surprise, and meaning.* Thousand Oaks, CA: Corwin Press.

Hord, S. M., & Sommers, W. A. (2008). *Leading professional learning communities: Voices from research and practice.* Thousand Oaks, CA: Corwin Press.

Johnson, D. W., & Johnson, R. T. (1989). *Cooperation and competition: Theory and research.* Edina, MN: Interaction Book.

Killion, J. (2008). *Assessing impact: Evaluating staff development* (2nd ed.). Thousand Oaks, CA: Corwin Press.

Killion, J., & Roy, P. (2009). *Becoming a learning school.* Oxford, OH: National Staff Development Council.

Kirkpatrick, D. (1998). *Evaluating training programs: The four levels.* San Francisco: Berrett–Koehler.

Lambert, L. (1998). *Building leadership capacity in schools.* Alexandria, VA: Association for Supervision and Curriculum Development.

Learning Forward. (2010). Definition of professional development. Accessed at www.learningforward.org/standfor/definition.cfm on March 17, 2011.

Lee, J. (2006). *Tracking achievement gaps and assessing the impact of NCLB on the gaps: An in-depth look into national and state reading and math outcome trends.* Cambridge, MA: The Civil Rights Project at Harvard University.

Lezotte, L. W., & McKee, K. M. (2002). *Assembly required: A continuous school improvement system.* Okemos, MI: Effective Schools.

Marzano, R. J. (2003). *What works in schools: Translating research into action.* Alexandria, VA: Association for Supervision and Curriculum Development.

Marzano, R. J., & Waters, T. (2009). *District leadership that works: Striking the right balance.* Bloomington, IN: Solution Tree Press.

Maslow, A. (1968). *Toward a psychology of being.* New York: Van Nostrand Reinhold.

Munger, L., & von Frank, V. (2010). *Change, lead, succeed: Building capacity with school leadership teams.* Oxford, OH: National Staff Development Council.

Newmann, F. M., & Wehlage, G. (1995). *Successful school restructuring: A report to the public and educators.* Madison, WI: Wisconsin Center for Educational Research.

O'Neill, J. (2008). System change can take education goals from fantasy to reality. *Journal of Staff Development, 29*(2), 48–50.

O'Neill, J., & Conzemius, A. (2006). *The power of SMART goals: Using goals to improve student learning.* Bloomington, IN: Solution Tree Press.

Osterman, K. F., & Kottkamp, R. B. (2004). *Reflective practice for educators: Professional development to improve student learning* (2nd ed.). Thousand Oaks, CA: Corwin Press.

Phillips, J. (1997). *Return on investment in training and performance improvement programs.* Houston, TX: Gulf.

Ragland, M. A., Asera, R., & Johnson, J. F. (1999). *Urgency, responsibility, efficacy: Preliminary findings of a study of high-performing Texas school districts.* Austin, TX: Dana Research Center.

Reeves, D. B. (2000). *Accountability in action: A blueprint for learning organizations.* Denver, CO: Advanced Learning Press.

Roy, P., & Hord, S. (2003). *Moving NSDC's staff development standards into practice: Innovation configurations.* Oxford, OH: National Staff Development Council.

Saphier, J., & D'Auria, J. (1993). *How to bring vision to school improvement: Through core outcomes, commitments and beliefs.* Carlisle, MA: Research for Better Teaching.

Saunders, W. M., Goldenberg, C. N., & Gallimore, R. (2009). Increasing achievement by focusing grade-level teams on improving classroom learning: A prospective, quasi-experimental study of Title I schools. *American Educational Research Journal, 46*(4), 1006–1033.

Schlechty, P. C. (1991). *Schools for the 21st century: Leadership imperatives for educational reform.* San Francisco: Jossey-Bass.

Senge, P. (1990). *The fifth discipline: The art and practice of the learning organization* (2nd ed.). New York: Doubleday.

Shrawder, J. H. (2006). *Planning a successful lesson.* Rio Rancho, NM: Pentronics.

Smith, I. (Producer), & Underwood, R. (Director). (1991). *City slickers* [Motion picture]. United States: Castle Rock Entertainment.

Spillane, J. P. (2005). Distributed leadership. *The Educational Forum, 69*(2), 143–150. Indianapolis, IN: Kappa Delta Pi. Accessed at http://course1.winona.edu/lgray/el756/Articles/Spillane.htm on March 16, 2011.

Stiggins, R., Arter, J., Chappuis, J., & Chappuis, S. (2007). *Classroom assessment for student learning: Doing it right—using it well.* Princeton, NJ: Merrill Prentice Hall.

van Manen, M. (2002). The pathic principle of pedagogical language. *Teaching and Teacher Education, 18*(2), 215–224.

Wang, M. C., Haertel, G. D., & Walberg, H. J. (1993). Toward a knowledge base for school learning. *Review of Educational Research, 63*(3), 249–294.

Wei, R. C., Darling-Hammond, L., & Adamson, F. (2010). *Professional development in the United States: Trends and challenges.* Dallas, TX: National Staff Development Council.

Weisbord, M. (1991). *Productive workplaces: Organizing and managing for dignity, meaning, and community.* San Francisco: Jossey-Bass.

Wellman, B., & Lipton, L. (2004). *Data-driven dialogue: A facilitator's guide to collaborative inquiry.* Sherman, CT: MiraVia.

Wheatley, M. J. (1992). *Leadership and the new science: Learning about organization from an orderly universe.* San Francisco: Berrett-Koehler.

Yoon, K. S., Duncan, T., Lee, S. W.-Y., Scarloss, B., & Shapley, K. L. (2007). *Reviewing the evidence on how teacher professional development affects student achievement* (Issues & Answers Report, REL 2007–No. 033). Washington, DC: U.S. Department of Education. Accessed at http://ies.ed.gov/ncee/edlabs/regions/southwest/pdf/REL_2007033.pdf on March 17, 2011.

York-Barr, J., Sommers, W. A., Ghere, G. S., & Montie, J. (2006). *Reflective practice to improve schools: An action guide for educators.* Thousand Oaks, CA: Corwin Press.

INDEX

The Power of SMART Goals:
Using Goals to Improve Student Learning
Jan O'Neill and Anne Conzemius
This easy-to-read guide will help your staff set effective goals that lead to real results. Four success stories illustrate how to transform challenges into opportunities for learning using an approach that is strategic and specific, measurable, attainable, results-based, and time-bound. That's SMART! **BKF207**

The Handbook for SMART School Teams
Anne Conzemius and Jan O'Neill
Learn what makes a school team SMART and how you can collaborate to achieve positive results. This practical, engaging handbook shares best practices essential to building a solid network of support. **BKF115**

Learning by Doing:
A Handbook for Professional Learning Communities at Work™
Richard DuFour, Rebecca DuFour, Robert Eaker, and Thomas Many
The second edition of *Learning by Doing* is an action guide for closing the knowing-doing gap and transforming schools into PLCs. It also includes seven major additions that equip educators with essential tools for confronting challenges. **BKF416**

Data Dynamics:
Aligning Teacher Team, School, and District Efforts
Edie L. Holcomb
Data are essential to guiding school improvement. Choosing the right data and using them well can be challenging, however. Explore common school scenarios that show how effective data teams work, and gain strategies for how to better use data to help all students succeed. Helpful protocols are included to guide data team work and discussions. **BKF424**